FAMOUS RACING CARS

FAMOUS RACING CARS

David Hodges

First published in Great Britain in 1962
by Temple Press Books Limited

This edition published in 2010 by Bounty Books,
a division of Octopus Publishing Group Ltd
Endeavour House,
189 Shaftesbury Avenue,
London WC2H 8JY
www.octopusbooks.co.uk

An Hachette UK Company
www.hachette.co.uk

Copyright © Octopus Publishing Group Ltd 2010

ISBN: 978-0-753719-91-6

A CIP catalogue record for this book is available from
the British Library

Printed and bound in China

PREFACE

Progress in racing and racing car design has never advanced steadily. Indeed, if all the many factors which might signify 'progress' in this context could be plotted on a graph, a very uneven line of development and improvement would result. Few machines in any period have successfully combined all the virtues of their time.

During the half-century covered by this book, the greatest single factor influencing racing car design has been the series of Formulae laid down by the governing body of the sport. Some of these have been derided, and on occasion ignored. Primarily intended in most cases to inhibit performance by limitations imposed on such factors as weight, engine capacity and fuel content or consumption, the official Formulae have, however, contained the rise in speed within manageable limits, and post-war Formulae have certainly produced much good racing and acted as an effective stimulus to design.

The end of a chapter in motor racing history has been deliberately chosen as the starting-point for this book, in order that one of the early road-racing giants might act as a yardstick by which to judge the advancing sophistication—and occasional backslidings—of the past fifty years. The emphasis has naturally been placed upon Grand Prix cars to the exclusion of many famous machines from the subsidiary classes.

In pursuit of these aims constant reference has been made to the files of *The Motor*. The two volumes of *The Grand Prix Car* have been another indispensable source of reference, and special thanks are due to its author Laurence Pomeroy. Further thanks are due to T. D. Collins for preparing the drawings. The following manufacturers and organizations also deserve acknowledgement for their assistance and for permission to reproduce their photographs: The Austin Motor Co. (p. 44); Automobiles Peugeot (pp. 4 and 8); Daimler Benz AG (p. 36); France-Reportage (p. 12); Louis Klemantaski Ltd. (p. 48); Libraries Hachette (p. 10), and Photo Meurisse (p. 6). The remaining pictures are from the files of *The Motor*.

Above all, the assistance so willingly given by Brian Cottee throughout the preparation of the book has been quite invaluable.

D.W.H.

CONTENTS

CONTENTS *continued*

Last of the giants, the 14-litre Fiat displays its heritage in the wooden-spoked wheels, side-chain final drive, rudimentary cockpit and, above all, sheer size. (Bruce Brown's car at the pits during the 1912 French Grand Prix at Dieppe.)

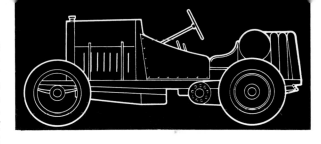

THE FIRST THREE French Grands Prix were won by direct descendants of the giants of the city-to-city races: by a 12·8-litre Renault in 1906, by a 16·2-litre Fiat in 1907 and, under regulations restricting engine size (roughly to a 155 mm. bore in a four-cylinder unit) for the first time, by a 12·8-litre Mercedes in 1908. However, the largest number of cubic centimetres did not even then guarantee success — the biggest of them all, the 18,279-c.c. Panhard, was not a serious challenger in the first Grand Prix. Although 14·1-litre Lorraine-Dietrichs and 12·5-litre 'Pilette' Mercedes, both with chain drive, were raced in 1913, the last effective road-racing giant was the 1912 14-litre Fiat prepared for the fourth French Grand Prix.

This was developed, through the fairly successful 1910–11 10-litre Type 61, from the 1908 G.P. car and retained all the archaic outward features characteristic of the Heroic Age. Under its enormous bonnet, however, it had an efficient o.h.c. engine. The cylinders were cast in two pairs with an integral head, on either side of which was an inlet and an exhaust valve, the pairs on opposite sides connected and operated by a single cam.

The three Fiats were undoubtedly the fastest cars entered for the 1912 Grand Prix—one was timed at 101·67 m.p.h.—during which ten laps of the 47·7-mile Dieppe course had to be covered on each of two consecutive days. At the end of the first day the American driver David Bruce Brown led in a Fiat at an average speed of 72·4 m.p.h., having put in the fastest lap of the race, 76·8 m.p.h. (1·7 m.p.h. below the 1908 record). He

retired on the second day, leaving his team-mate Wagner to finish over 13 minutes behind Boillot's Peugeot at an average speed of 67·32 m.p.h. Third was a 3-litre Sunbeam, 27½ minutes down on Wagner after 14½ hours' racing. The next giant, Christiaens' Excelsior, finished sixth, nearly 2½ hours after the winner. An era ended with a whimper. . . .

SPECIFICATION

Engine: 4 cylinders; 150 × 200 mm.; 14,137 c.c.; single o.h.c.; max. power: 140 b.h.p. at 1,700 r.p.m. (9·9 b.h.p. per litre).
Frame: Channel.
Suspension: Front: rigid axle and semi-elliptics; rear: dead axle and semi-elliptics.
Brakes: Mechanical drum (rear only).
Dimensions: Wheelbase: 8 ft. 11 in.; track, front and rear, 4 ft. 5 in.

4 *The 200-mm. piston stroke and tall overhead-camshaft valvegear of the 7·6-litre Peugeot enforced a high build, but its uninspiring appearance concealed technical advances which set a new pattern. (Goux at Indianapolis, 1913.)*

PEUGEOT 7·6-litre

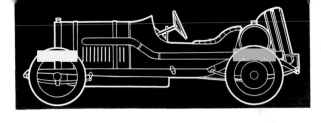

MORE THAN ANY other machine, the 7·6-litre 1912 Peugeot marks the boundary between ancient and modern in racing cars: it dealt the final blow to the multi-litre giants of the Heroic Age, represented a fresh school of design which dominated racing for a decade, and introduced features that have remained current to the present day.

When Grand Prix racing was resumed in 1912 after a break of three years (largely brought about by the manufacturers' boycott) Peugeot, who had hitherto competed only in light-car events, were persuaded by their drivers Boillot, Goux and Zuccarelli to produce a car based on preliminary work done for the abortive 1911 Grand Prix. Ernest Henri, a young Swiss engineer, was enlisted to create a car representing a rejection of the 'more litres for more power' principle—even though the 1912 race was to be an unlimited-capacity event. Not strikingly novel in appearance, Henri's car was nevertheless a remarkable technical advance, especially since he inherited the long-stroke (110 × 200 mm.) cylinder dimensions intended for the 1911 engine. Two overhead camshafts were used for the first time and were combined with four inclined valves per cylinder and hemispherical combustion chambers. To relieve the fragile valve-springs of those days, the tappets had stirrup ends which encircled the cams and had their own 'helper' return springs. The cylinder block and head were a single iron casting, offset in relation to the one-piece crankshaft to reduce piston-thrust losses. The engine, which drove through a remote close-ratio gearbox, was mounted on a separate sub-frame isolated from chassis flexions by ball-and-socket joints. Enormous (18 in.) drum brakes on the rear wheels were supplemented by a transmission brake.

The car won the only two G.P. races of 1912. In the French Grand Prix at Dieppe, Boillot finished well ahead of the big Fiat; two months later Goux won the confusingly-titled 'Grand Prix de France' on the Sarthe circuit and in the following year he drove the 7·6-litre Peugeot to victory in the 500-mile race at Indianapolis, at 75·9 m.p.h.—the first win for a European car.

SPECIFICATION

Engine: 4 cylinders; 110 × 200 mm.; 7,600 c.c.; twin o.h.c.; max. power: 135 b.h.p. at 2,200 r.p.m. (17·8 b.h.p. per litre).
Frame: Channel.
Suspension: Front: rigid axle and semi-elliptics; rear: live axle and semi-elliptics. Friction shock absorbers.
Brakes: Mechanical drum (rear wheels and transmission only).
Dimensions: Wheelbase: 9 ft. 1 in.; track, front and rear, 4 ft. 6 in.

SUNBEAM 3-litre

With spoked metal wheels, rounded radiators and slim, tapered bodies, the 1912 Sunbeams had an out-of-period appearance, seeming to modern eyes to belong more to the 'twenties. (Médinger, behind tail, refuelling at the Dieppe pits, 1912.)

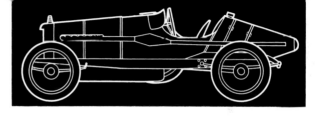

PRESENT-DAY MEMORIES of British racing successes seldom reach back farther than Segrave's 1923 French G.P. victory with a Sunbeam. But the same marque triumphed on the Continent eleven years earlier when three cars driven by Victor Rigal, Dario Resta and M. Médinger not only took first three places in the 1912 Coupe de *l'Auto* race for 3-litre machines and won the team prize, but were beaten only by one 7·6-litre and one 14·1-litre car in the unlimited-capacity Grand Prix run concurrently. And this in a race with forty-seven starters.

The annual Coupe de *l'Auto* races, for voiturettes and light cars, were roughly equivalent to a Formula 2, and the Sunbeams which ran in them for several seasons were based very closely on the 12/16 h.p. production model, although they owed something to the cars which had run regularly at Brooklands, where their especial rivals were Vauxhalls (which proved fast but unreliable at Dieppe in 1912). Louis Coatalen, the Sunbeam designer, said, 'Brooklands enabled us to gain this victory'; and probably stability as well as sustained speed (on only 75 b.h.p.) came from experience on the British track, while the reliability of the long-stroke, four-cylinder, side-valve engines was an outstanding feature of the race. Running with a 3,000 r.p.m. rev. limit, the two leading cars finished in 14½ hours without any trouble (Médinger, delayed by a punctured petrol tank, took 16 hours), lapping at around 65 m.p.h. and touching 95 m.p.h. downhill on the loose-surfaced circuit outside Dieppe.

The slim 3-litre Sunbeams were mechanically conventional, having semi-elliptic suspension for rigid front and rear axles, a leather-faced cone clutch and a four-speed gearbox, but they were small and light (less than a ton all-up) compared with the G.P. cars. They represented the peak of the side-valve in international formula racing, for by the following year the comparatively more powerful o.h.c. cars had found reliability as well. In the 1913 race, at Boulogne, the Sunbeams were too slow despite interim development and streamlined nose fairings, and only Lee Guinness's virtuosity gained them a third place.

SPECIFICATION

Engine: 4 cylinders; 80 × 148·7 mm.; 2.986 c.c.; side valves; max. power: 75 b.h.p. at 2,800 r.p.m. (25·1 b.h.p. per litre).
Frame: Channel.
Suspension: Front: rigid axle and semi-elliptics; rear: live axle and semi-elliptics. Friction shock absorbers.
Brakes: Mechanical drum (rear wheels and transmission only).
Dimensions: Wheelbase: 8 ft. 11 in.; track, front and rear, 4 ft. 6 in.

8 *The 1913 Peugeot twin-cam 3-litre not only dominated its own class of racing but successfully challenged the Grand Prix cars. (Boillot's 1913 Coupe de l' Auto car.)*

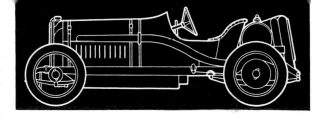

ALTHOUGH ONE OF Henri's 7·6-litre twin-o.h.c. Pcugeots won the 1912 Grand Prix, his 3-litre prototype in the concurrent Coupe de *l'Auto* section of the race made no impression. This he remedied in the following year, not only producing a 5·6-litre G.P. winner on the same general lines as in 1912, but developing his 3-litre into a race-winning car which spelt the end of the side-valve in all classes of serious racing.

Lower built and much lighter (about 15 cwt. dry) than the 7·6-litre car, the 1913 3-litre was nevertheless very similar in layout and—apart from a neater body and tapered radiator—in appearance. Engine design, too, was on the same lines, with stirrups encircling the cams of the twin-o.h.c. valvegear to withdraw the tappets positively (but not to close the valves). The valves were splayed from 45° (in 1912) to 60°, and at 78 × 156 mm. the bore was exactly half the stroke.

The novel counterbalanced crankshaft was made in two parts, bolted together, and ran in ball bearings. The crankcase was a one-piece casting with a central web carrying the centre main bearing and was thus exceptionally rigid. These features contributed to the 3-litre's undoubted reliability, offsetting the effects of a rather crude dry-sump lubrication system. Engine, cone clutch and close-ratio four-speed gearbox were mounted on a separate sub-frame.

When this modified 3-litre appeared in September 1913 it gave Georges Boillot, fresh from success with the 5·6-litre at Amiens, a runaway win in the 388-mile Coupe de *l'Auto* at Boulogne, followed home by Goux on a sister car which set the lap record at 65·5 m.p.h. Behind them were Lee Guinness on a Sunbeam and Hancock on a Vauxhall. One of the Peugeots was entered privately in the 1914 Indianapolis '500', where Duray drove it into second place, beating two 5·6-litre works Peugeots (ironically, Boillot and Goux) and other large G.P. cars.

Although it won no more classic races, Henri's 3-litre influenced design for many years and was moral victor in the 1914 T.T., where the winning Sunbeams were almost carbon copies of it.

SPECIFICATION

Engine: 4 cylinders; 78 × 156 mm.; 2,980 c.c.; twin o.h.c.; max. power: 90 b.h.p. at 2,950 r.p.m. (30·2 b.h.p. per litre).
Frame: Channel.
Suspension: Front: rigid axle and semi-elliptics; rear: live axle and semi-elliptics. Friction shock absorbers.
Brakes: Mechanical drum (rear wheels and transmission only).
Dimensions: Wheelbase: 9 ft. 4 in.; track, front and rear, 4 ft. 8½ in.

10 *Lautenschlager passes the main stand at Lyons during the 1914 Grand Prix. The generally clean lines—pointed radiator, tapered bonnet and partly enclosed spare wheels—suggest that some effort was made to reduce wind resistance.*

MERCEDES 4·5-Litre 1914

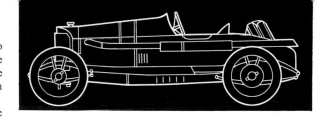

AFTER A LAPSE of six years, Mercedes officially returned to racing in 1914 with the immediate objective of victory in the Grand Prix de l'A.C.F. To this end their preparations were exceptionally thorough and in at least one respect, team control, set a pattern for future racing.

Built to the new Grand Prix Formula which limited engine capacity to 4½ litres and car weight to 21 cwt., the cars were conservative in basic design. Paul Daimler, the designer, followed the general 'rules' laid down by Henri, whilst the four-cylinder engine also owed much to Mercedes' aircraft engine experience, the cylinders being made individually and welded together (thus reviving an almost discarded practice which was later taken up by many other manufacturers). Each cylinder had four valves, driven by a single overhead camshaft, and provision for four plugs, although in practice only three were used. The engine was mounted directly on to the frame which was crossbraced beneath the cockpit and dropped between the wheels. Brakes were fitted on the rear wheels only.

In the Grand Prix the team fully achieved its aim, Christian Lautenschlager leading Wagner and Salzer in a Mercedes 1, 2, 3 victory at an average speed of more than 65 m.p.h. over twenty laps of the undulating, twisting 23·3-mile Lyons circuit. Their principal rival, Georges Boillot (Peugeot), fell out when in second place on the last lap but in the Peugeot-Mercedes duels on American tracks in 1915 and 1916 the German car scored only two wins—one in a minor track race

and the other at Indianapolis in 1915 when Ralph de Palma won the 500 Mile Sweepstake at 89·94 m.p.h.

Still competitive after the First World War—albeit refined to the extent of having brakes on all four wheels—the cars were raced almost throughout the twenties, their most notable win coming in the 1922 Targa Florio, and their general design formed the basis of a series of famous Mercedes sports cars.

SPECIFICATION

Engine: 4 cylinders; 93 × 165 mm.; 4,483 c.c.; single o.h.c.; max. power: 115 b.h.p. at 2,700–2,800 r.p.m. (25·6 b.h.p. per litre).

Frame: Channel.

Suspension: Front: rigid axle and semi-elliptics; rear: live axle and semi-elliptics. Coil spring shock absorbers.

Brakes: Mechanical drum (rear wheels and transmission only).

Dimensions: Wheelbase: 9 ft. 4 in.; track, front, 4 ft. 4½ in., rear, 4 ft. 5 in.

12 *The 1920 Ballot had a handsome and efficient body with low frontal area, faired-in tail and full undertray. (Chassagne, Le Mans, 1921.)*

BALLOT 3-litre

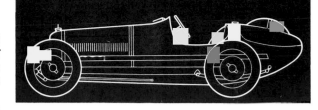

ETABLISSEMENTS BALLOT built cars between 1919 and 1931 and officially supported racing for only the first four of these years. But their G.P. cars introduced a new phase in motor sport, for they produced the first successful European straight-eight racing engine.

During the First World War, Bugatti had designed an eight-in-line aircraft engine which was put into production by Bara in France and Duesenberg in the U.S.A. An employee of the Bara company at that time was Ernest Henri, designer of the pre-war Peugeots, and when he accepted Ballot's invitation to design a car for the 1919 Indianapolis 500—four cars actually had to be built from scratch in less than four months!—he naturally drew upon his wartime experience with the Bugatti engine.

Installed in a near-replica of the 1913 Peugeot, his first straight-eight had a capacity of 4·9 litres. It was raced in only one major event, the 1919 '500' (although Count Zborowski's car later became familiar to Brooklands racegoers), for a capacity limit of 3 litres, common to both Europe and America, was announced for 1920–21. For this Formula, Henri produced a scaled-down version of the engine, reducing the bore and stroke by 9 × 28 mm. Light-alloy pistons and crankcase followed the Bugatti practice, whilst the single-plunger pump lubrication system, four valves per cylinder and gear-driven o.h.c. were reminiscent of the Peugeots, although the Ballot valves were enclosed. A weak big-end design, which included a bronze bush running in contact with steel, com-bined with the rudimentary lubrication system to impose a modest upper limit on engine speed.

This car was well in the lead after 465 miles of the 1920 Indianapolis race when it caught fire, eventually finishing second (third in 1922). Ballots failed again at Indianapolis in 1921, but finished second and third in the French Grand Prix at Le Mans (de Palma, Goux) and first and second (Goux, Chassagne) in the first Italian Grand Prix.

SPECIFICATION

Engine: 8 cylinders; 65 × 112 mm.; 2,960 c.c.; twin o.h.c.; max. power: 107 b.h.p. at 3,800 r.p.m. (36·1 b.h.p. per litre).

Frame: Channel.

Suspension: Front: rigid axle and semi-elliptics; rear: live axle and semi-elliptics. Friction shock absorbers.

Brakes: Mechanical drum.

Dimensions: Wheelbase: 8 ft. 8½ in.; track, front and rear, 4 ft. 4½ in.

14 *The rakish, long-tailed Grand Prix Duesenberg differed basically from European contemporaries in having left-hand drive and hydraulic brakes. (Boyer at Le Mans, 1921.)*

DUESENBERG 3-litre

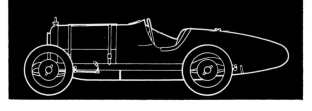

THE DUESENBERG BROTHERS, August and Frederick, shared with Ballot the distinction of successfully introducing the racing straight-eight. Unlike the French firm, however, they had a racing tradition to maintain—their four-cylinder cars had done well at Indianapolis before America entered the First World War (10th in the 1914 '500'; 5th and 8th in 1915; 2nd in 1916).

Their first straight-eight was built for the 1919 Indianapolis race, where it met the Ballot engine based on the same Bugatti design. Among its features were: a crankcase and block cast in one and with a detachable head; a shaft and bevel gears to drive the o.h.c. which operated three valves (one cam using a forked rocker to operate both exhaust valves); and a three-bearing built-up crankshaft and tubular connecting-rods (initially a weak point). When the Indianapolis Formula was reduced to 183 cu. in. in 1920, thus coinciding with the 1921–22 European 3-litre Formula, bore and stroke were reduced by 12·5 × 16 mm. It was the first G.P. car to use hydraulically-operated brakes, on the rear wheels only at Indianapolis but on all four for the 1921 visit to Europe.

The three cars which ran at Indianapolis in 1919 retired; Duesenbergs finished 3rd, 4th and 6th in the 1920 '500'; 2nd, 4th, 6th and 8th in 1921. Two of these were in the four-car team entered in the 1921 French Grand Prix—the first American starters since 1908 (Strang's Thomas)—when Jimmy Murphy staggered Europeans by winning comfortably at 78·1 m.p.h., setting a Le Mans lap record of 83·2 m.p.h. which was to stand for eight years. Dubonnet finished 4th; Boyer and Guyot retired. The brothers did not return to Europe, but their cars remained in the forefront at Indianapolis for another decade. Seven Duesenbergs finished in the first ten in the last 183 cu. in. '500' (and the winner used a Duesenberg chassis). The first Duesenberg win came in 1924 (Coram and Boyer in a 2-litre, twin-o.h.c. centrifugally-supercharged car), and in 1925 the winning Duesenberg (De Paolo and Batten) averaged 101·13 m.p.h.—over 100 m.p.h. for the first time at Indianapolis.

SPECIFICATION

Engine: 8 cylinders; 63.5 × 117 mm.; 2,964 c.c.; single o.h.c.; max. power; 115 b.h.p. at 4,225 r.p.m. (38.8 b.h.p. per litre).
Frame: Channel.
Suspension: Front: rigid axle and semi-elliptics; rear: live axle and semi-elliptics. Friction shock absorbers.
Brakes: Hydraulic drum.
Dimensions: Wheelbase: 8 ft. 10 in.; track, front and rear, 4 ft. 3 in.

16 *The slim, neat bodywork of the Type 804 Fiat set new standards. (Biagio Nazzaro, nephew of Felice, before the 1922 French Grand Prix in which he was killed.)*

FIAT TYPE 804 2-litre

JUST AS IN 1912 the Peugeot firmly marked the beginning of a new school of racing-car design, so ten years later did the six-cylinder Fiat 804 designed by Fornaca and his team for the new 2-litre Grand Prix Formula. Small, neat and light (some 5 cwt. lighter than the 3-litre cars of the previous year), the Fiats dominated the opening year of this very fruitful formula —yet they ran in only two races.

The engine of the 804 came directly from the 1921 3-litre straight-eight, having the same bore and a similar one-piece crankshaft and roller bearings for mains and big-ends; the latter had split bearing caps—a rare feature. The cylinders were welded into two in-line blocks of three, dry-sump lubrication was used and the alloy pistons carried steel rings designed for replacement after each race. The chassis was unusual in tapering inwards with the body at the rear (a much-copied feature) and the front leaf springs passed through slots in the tubular axle.

Three cars were entered for the 1922 French Grand Prix—the first massed-start G.P. ever held—at Strasbourg, and although two of them lost wheels (apparently through a weakness in the novel rear axle, which was welded-up from light steel pressings) the veteran Felice Nazzaro in the third car won from a Bugatti by nearly an hour in 500 miles. The pace of the Fiats had reduced the field to a shambles.

At Strasbourg the engines gave 95 b.h.p. at 4,500 r.p.m. and for the year's only other Grand Prix—on the new Italian track at Monza—the power was raised to 112 b.h.p. at 5,000 r.p.m. News of the Fiat entry had a devastating effect. Although many and various reasons were given for the non-starting of Ballot, Benz, Bianchi, Delage, Mercedes, Rolland-Pilain and Talbot-Darracq, this wholesale defection is ascribed to Fiat's obvious superiority. As a result, Bordino and Nazzaro had a walkover, the former averaging 86·89 m.p.h. and lapping at well over 90 m.p.h.

The 804's lines and layout were widely copied by rival marques, but its Fiat successor—the Type 405 straight-eight, which introduced the supercharger to Grand Prix racing—was far less successful, although it did win the 1924 Italian Grand Prix.

SPECIFICATION

Engine: 6 cylinders; 65 × 100 mm.; 1,991 c.c.; twin o.h.c.; max. power: 112 b.h.p. at 5,000 r.p.m. (59·8 b.h.p. per litre).
Frame: Channel.
Suspension: Front: rigid axle and semi-elliptics; rear: live axle and semi-elliptics. Friction shock absorbers.
Brakes: Mechanical drum.
Dimensions: Wheelbase: 8 ft. 2½ in.; track, front and rear, 3 ft. 11½ in.

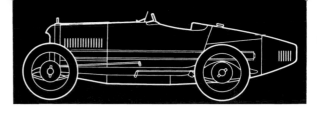

BY ENGAGING ERNEST HENRI to design their first 2-litre Grand Prix car Sunbeam might quite reasonably have expected to get a winner. However, he chose to abandon the straight-eight in favour of a four-cylinder engine, and thus gave away nearly 10 b.h.p. and 10 m.p.h. per lap to the Fiat 804s in the 1922 French Grand Prix (where in any case the three Sunbeams retired with valve failures).

Louis Coatalen thereupon persuaded one of the designers of the 804, Vincent Bertarione, to collaborate in the design of a new G.P. Sunbeam for 1923. Not surprisingly the new cars were more than superficially similar to the 1922 Fiats. In fact, the engine—perforce installed in Henri's chassis—differed only in detail (closer bore/stroke ratio and exhaust valve larger than inlet) and in its use of British ancillary components. It produced 103 b.h.p. at 5,500 r.p.m., 20 b.h.p. less than the new Fiat which the Sunbeams met at Tours in the French Grand Prix. They were, however, little slower and infinitely more reliable—this quality ensuring de Hane Segrave's famous victory (followed by his team-mates Divo and Guinness, 2nd and 4th). Later in the year Divo took one car to Sitges to win the first Spanish Grand Prix.

The cars were completely rebuilt for 1924. Henri's basic chassis and running gear were retained; wheelbase and track were increased, and supercharging introduced to increase power and to even out the power curve throughout the r.p.m. range (for the first time on a European car the supercharger was used to compress mixture). In this form they were un-doubtedly the fastest cars entered for the French Grand Prix, but constant misfiring resulting from a last-minute magneto change cost them the race (Segrave finished 5th, raising the Lyons lap record to 76·1 m.p.h., and Resta 9th). Segrave's Spanish G.P. win two months later partly compensated Sunbeams for this defeat. In 1925, the last 2-litre G.P. season, Count Masetti was 3rd in the French Grand Prix, retired at San Sebastian and made f.t.d. at Klausen. The cars continued to compete consistently and successfully in British events.

SPECIFICATION (1924)

Engine: 6 cylinders; 67 × 94 mm.; 1,988 c.c.; twin o.h.c.; Roots-type supercharger; max. power: 138 b.h.p. at 5,500 r.p.m. (69·4 b.h.p. per litre).
Frame: Channel.
Suspension: Front: rigid axle and semi-elliptics; rear: live axle and semi-elliptics. Friction shock absorbers.
Brakes: Mechanical drum.
Dimensions: Wheelbase: 8 ft. 6 in.; track, front, 4 ft. 5 in., rear, 4 ft. 1 in.

20 *The first successful Grand Prix V-12, the 1924 Delage, had a well-proportioned and smooth body. The 1925 supercharged version (drawing) had numerous extra bonnet louvres. (Benoist, no. 15, leads Thomas in the 1924 French Grand Prix.)*

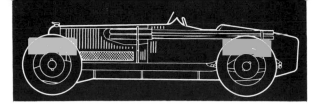

HARD ON THE heels of the successful racing straight-eights came the V-12 Delage, a sophisticated and advanced design which in two years developed into a remarkably effective contender. Louis Delage had built his first Grand Prix car in 1913 (winner at Indianapolis, 1914), ignored the first post-war formula and almost returned to racing with a four-cylinder 2-litre in 1922. This, however, was a consistent non-starter and was scrapped, to be replaced in 1923 by the hastily-built Plancton V-12.

When other designers were turning to supercharging in their search for power, Plancton chose the alternative of high piston area (38·7 sq. in. compared with the contemporary Sunbeam's 32·9) and the promise of high r.p.m., in practice obtaining 120 b.h.p. at 6,000 r.p.m. The one-piece crankshaft was machined from the solid, and auxiliaries and the camshafts, two to each bank, were gear-driven from the front. The exhaust manifolds were between the banks, emerging high on the mechanic's side.

The V-12 was hardly completed for the 1923 French Grand Prix, René Thomas bringing one car to the line and staying with the leaders for a few laps before retiring with over-heating. At Lyons in the following year Delages finished second third and sixth, beaten by the supercharged P.2, and in the Spanish Grand Prix Morel and Divo were third and fourth behind Segrave's Sunbeam and a Bugatti.

By this time development had been taken over by A. Lory (designer of the V-8 engine of France's 1947 white elephant, the C.T.A.-Arsenal), who recognized the virtues of forced induction and used twin superchargers to raise engine output above 190 b.h.p. for 1925. In their first 1925 race four Delages faced three Alfa Romeos in the G.P. de l'Europe at Spa. By half-distance one P.2 and all the Delages were out of the race (Benoist with a split tank, Divo and Torchy with 'plug trouble', whilst Thomas crashed). In the French Grand Prix Benoist/Divo and Wagner/Torchy finished first and second after the withdrawal of the Alfa Romeo team and the V-12 wound up its career with a runaway 1, 2, 3 victory (Divo, Benoist, Thomas) in the Spanish Grand Prix at San Sebastian.

SPECIFICATION

Engine: 12 cylinders (60° V-12); 51·3 × 80 mm.; 1,992 c.c.; twin o.h.c.; two Roots-type superchargers; max. power: 195 b.h.p. at 7,000 r.p.m. (97·9 b.h.p. per litre).

Frame: Channel.

Suspension: Front: rigid axle and semi-elliptics; rear: live axle and semi-elliptics. Friction shock absorbers.

Brakes: Mechanical drum.

Dimensions: Wheelbase: 8 ft. 6 in.; track, front and rear, 4 ft. 2 in.

22 *The Alfa Romeo P.2 won its first race and was the dominant design in the last two years of the 2-litre Formula. (Antonio Ascari, father of Alberto, before the 1925 French Grand Prix, in which he was killed.)*

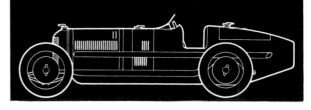

THE FIRST ALFA ROMEO Grand Prix car, the six-cylinder supercharged P.1 built in 1923, was never actually raced and was replaced by the completely new P.2 in 1924.

The P.2 was designed by Vittorio Jano (previously employed by Fiat) and its supercharged straight-eight engine followed Fiat practice in having four welded-together pairs of steel cylinders. The crankshaft and big ends ran on roller bearings and the permanently-engaged supercharger was driven from the front of the crankshaft, forcing air back through a pipe to the carburetter at the rear of the engine. This developed about 155 b.h.p. when the car was introduced, power for which the chassis and running gear were just adequate (they were considerably modified when the cars were raced in 1928–30 with the output of their engines increased by some 40 b.h.p.).

After winning the first race for which it was entered (at Cremona) the P.2 driven by Campari won the 1924 French Grand Prix and the Alfa Romeo team went on to a 1, 2, 3 victory in the Italian Grand Prix, Antonio Ascari setting a Monza lap record of 104·24 m.p.h. which was to stand for six years. In 1925 the cars took first and second places in the Belgian and Italian Grands Prix and were leading the French Grand Prix at Montlhéry when they were withdrawn after Ascari's fatal accident.

During the two years of the subsequent 1·5-litre Formula the P.2s appeared in occasional *Formule Libre* events, but when most organizers decided to ignore the 1928–30 Formulae

and run free-for-all races the cars were revamped and raced by independents, occasionally by the factory and, in 1930, by a new team, Scuderia Ferrari. Generally they followed Bugattis past the chequered flag, but in 1928 Campari won at Pescara and Enzo Ferrari at Modena. In 1929 they won another five races and in 1930 Varzi drove single-handed to break the Bugatti Targa Florio monopoly, winning at the record average of 48·48 m.p.h., and winning one other secondary race.

SPECIFICATION

Engine: 8 cylinders; 61 × 85 mm.; 1,987 c.c.; twin o.h.c.; Roots-type supercharger; max. power: 155 b.h.p. at 5,500 r.p.m. (78 b.h.p. per litre).

Frame: Channel.

Suspension: Front: rigid axle and semi-elliptics; rear: live axle and semi-elliptics. Friction shock absorbers.

Brakes: Mechanical drum.

Dimensions: Wheelbase: 8 ft. 6 in.; track, front, 4 ft. 5 in., rear, 4 ft. 1 in.

24 *Most successful car of the 1928–30 free-formula Grands Prix, the Type 35 Bugatti in its various forms was the only really competitive machine available to private owners. (P. de Viscaya before the start of the 1925 French Grand Prix.)*

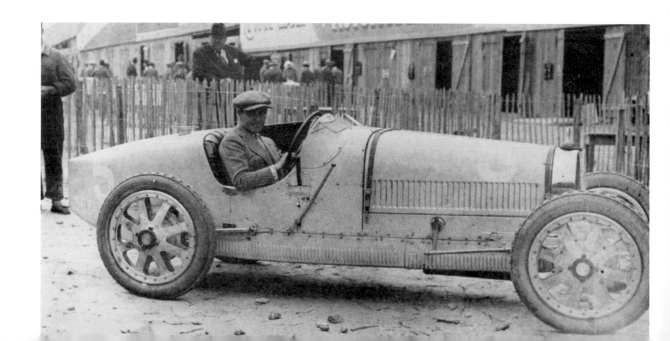

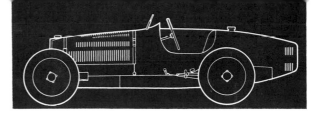

BUGATTI'S CLASSIC TYPE 35 was in the front rank of racing for seven years and was perhaps his only G.P. car fully to merit the adoration accorded to the marque today. During these years it was actually in production (the first catalogued G.P. car), becoming far and away the most widely-used and successful Grand Prix car built before the Second World War.

The chassis and running gear, altered only in detail between 1924 and 1931, gave the car outstanding roadholding which more than compensated for the comparatively modest output of its engine. The frame was extremely rigid, with main members varying in depth (from ¾ in. at their extremities to 6¾ in. at the centre) to match stress variations and stiffened transversely by the engine and by tubes at the back. Bugatti used his 'standard' rear suspension (reversed quarter-elliptics balanced by radius arms to take drive torque) and unique light alloy wheels with flat spokes and integral brake drums—efficient but odd when wire wheels had been a *sine qua non* for many years.

The general features of the straight-eight engine had been conceived in 1914 and similar units had powered the 1922–23 G.P. cars. Bugatti at first eschewed supercharging, but introduced it in the Type 39 variant built for the 1926–27 Formula and retained it in the Types 35B (2·3 litres) and 35C (2 litres), the supercharger being mounted on the offside and gear-driven from the front. The engine—indeed, the whole car—displayed the precision and craftsmanship for which Molsheim was renowned.

The Type 35 gained no major successes in 1924 and only one, the first of five consecutive Targa Florio wins, in 1925. The Type 39 won the French (unopposed at Miramas) and Spanish Grands Prix in 1926. Then the 35B and 35C enjoyed three outstandingly successful seasons, winning the Grands Prix of France (1929 and 1930); Belgium (1930); Italy (1928); Monaco (1929 and 1930) and Spain (1928 and 1929); many secondary races and literally hundreds of minor events.

SPECIFICATION (TYPE 35C)

Engine: 8 cylinders; 60 × 88 mm.; 1,955 c.c.; single o.h.c.; Roots-type supercharger; max. power: 135 b.h.p. at 5,300 r.p.m. (69 b.h.p. per litre).

Frame: Channel.

Suspension: Front: rigid axle and semi-elliptics; rear: live axle, quarter-elliptics and radius arms. Friction shock absorbers.

Brakes: Mechanical drum.

Dimensions: Wheelbase: 7 ft. 10 in.; track, front, 4 ft. 1 in., rear, 3 ft. 11 in.

26 *Low-built G.P. cars are no recent innovation: the straight-eight Delage had a body little higher than its wheels. The transmission passed alongside the driver. (Before the 1927 British G.P. at Brooklands; left to right, Bourlier, 2nd in the race, Benoist, 1st, and Divo, 3rd.)*

DELAGE 1·5-litre

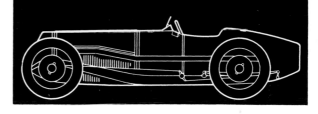

FOR RACES UNDER the 1926–27 Formula (1·5 litres, minimum weight 700 kg.) Delage abandoned their V-12 car, replacing it with an outstanding supercharged straight-eight.

The remarkably efficient (but heavy) engine made extensive use of roller bearings, the crankshaft running in nine whilst the big ends and auxiliary drives used a further thirty-nine. In 1926 it gave 160 b.h.p., in 1927 170 b.h.p. (114 b.h.p. per litre—roughly as much as the W.125 Mercedes) and nearly a decade later almost 200 b.h.p. 'on the bench'. Forming a long, thin unit with the gearbox, this engine was installed at a slight angle in the light, flexible chassis.

The car proved very fast in its first race, an asset nullified by frequent pit stops to change and cool drivers, for the very hot exhaust running within inches of their feet made cockpit conditions almost unendurable on an already hot Spanish July day. Two pairs of drivers (Senechal/Wagner, Benoist/Dubonnet) nevertheless managed to finish first and third in the first British Grand Prix at Brooklands in the following month.

To overcome this embarrassing drawback Lory radically modified the car for 1927, reversing the cylinder block so that the exhaust ran along the nearside, this in turn meaning that the centrally-placed superchargers had to be replaced by a single larger unit mounted behind the radiator. In this form the Delage proved unbeatable. It finished first, second and third in the French and British Grands Prix, first and third in the Spanish Grand Prix and the sole car entered for the Italian Grand Prix won by over twenty minutes.

Thereafter the cars were raced by independents, notably Malcolm Campbell, Earl Howe, W. B. Scott and Chiron, who took one to Indianapolis in 1929 and finished seventh. The ex-Chiron Howe car was bought by Dick Seaman and, virtually rebuilt by Giulio Ramponi, became a formidable voiturette contender in 1936, winning, *inter alia*, on three consecutive week-ends at Pescara, Berne and Donington. Its next owner, Bira, seldom used it, although he further modernized it by fitting i.f.s., but after the war (with another car built up from parts by Parnell) it was again actively raced, eventually with an E.R.A. engine, by several drivers.

SPECIFICATION

Engine: 8 cylinders; 55·8 × 76 mm.; 1,488 c.c.; twin o.h.c.; single Roots-type supercharger; max. power: 170 b.h.p. at 8,000 r.p.m. (114·2 b.h.p. per litre).

Frame: Channel.

Suspension: Front: rigid axle and semi-elliptics; rear: live axle and semi-elliptics. Friction shock absorbers.

Brakes: Mechanical drum.

Dimensions: Wheelbase: 8 ft. 2½ in.; track, front and rear, 4 ft. 5 in.

28 *One of the first true single-seaters (monoposto), with its cockpit astride the centre-line, the P.3 looked every inch a thoroughbred. (Trossi waiting to practise, Monaco, 1934.)*

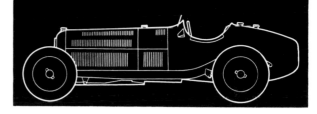

THE PERSONIFICATION OF the classic Grand Prix car, Vittorio Jano's Alfa Romeo Type B 'Monoposto'—P.3 to all but the most pedantic—replaced the unsatisfactory Type A 'twin-six' and underpowered 8C 'Monza' in 1932 and incorporated some of the best features from both.

The 8C's straight-eight engine was used, enlarged from 2·3 to 2·65 litres (B-2600), then to 2·9 litres (B-2900) and finally, as a rearguard stopgap in the face of Teutonic might, to 3·2 and 3·8 litres. It had two blocks of four cylinders, a one-piece cylinder head and a two-piece crankshaft joined through a train of gears between the blocks. These drove the camshafts and two superchargers, each feeding one set of cylinders. The transmission was developed from the twin propeller shaft layout of the Type A. Immediately behind the engine-gearbox unit was the differential, from which two angled propeller shafts took the power to twin bevel final drives, one at each end of the axle. The low weight of the car—15·2 cwt.—in part compensated for the modest power of the engine.

The P.3 won its first race, the Italian G.P., and was defeated only twice during the rest of its first season. Alfa Romeo then withdrew from racing, leaving Scuderia Ferrari to uphold the honour of the marque with bored-out 8Cs. Only in August 1933, when these cars were losing too frequently, were the P.3s handed over to Ferrari to enjoy another run of successes.

The B-2900 was introduced for the 750-kg. Formula which came into effect in 1934, but was soon demoted to obsolescence by two formidable German cars, holding its own only while Mercedes-Benz and Auto Union sorted out their teething troubles. But, until new Italian cars could be built, the P.3 lingered on in first-class racing, Nuvolari's fantastic victory against odds in the 1935 German Grand Prix coming as a last flash of glory.

SPECIFICATION

Engine: 8 cylinders; 65 × 100 mm.; 2,653 c.c.; twin o.h.c.; two Roots-type superchargers; max. power: 190 b.h.p. at 5,400 r.p.m. (71·6 b.h.p. per litre).
Frame: Channel.
Suspension: Front: rigid axle and semi-elliptics; rear: rigid axle and semi-elliptics. Friction shock absorbers.
Brakes: Mechanical drum.
Dimensions: Wheelbase: 8 ft. 6 in.; track, front and rear, 4 ft. 5 in.

30 *Introduced to Britain by Whitney Straight in 1934, the 2·9 Maserati had a long and useful life in the British front rank. (B. Bira, Campbell Trophy, Brooklands, 1939).*

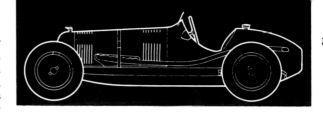

THE BROTHERS MASERATI built the first racing car to bear their name in 1926. This car, a supercharged 1·5-litre based on their G.P. Diatto design, was followed by a machine in which coupled eight-cylinder engines were installed side-by-side, the resultant 16-cylinder being a little more successful than its near-contemporaries which adopted the same rather clumsy layout. Then, in 1930, their 2·5-litre straight-eight ended the three-year period of sterility in racing-car design, the reward for this enterprise coming in seven race victories. A 2·8-litre derivative kept pace with the Alfa Romeos and (after a brief Maserati flirtation with front-wheel drive) the design was further developed in the 1933 2·9-litre monoposto. This car was in the forefront on the Continent until the German on-slaught changed the face of racing, and became well known on British circuits between 1934 and 1939.

The supercharged twin-o.h.c. engine broke no new ground and the narrow chassis, with its main members dropped be-tween the wheels, was conventional. However, hydraulic brakes were fitted to all four wheels of a European racing car for the first time (Duesenberg had set the precedent in the early twenties). The body was less upright than those of other 1933 cars, very slim in that year and widened to comply with the 750-kg. Formula regulations in 1934.

The car made its racing début at Tunis in 1932 and in 1933 showed itself to be faster, but less reliable, than the P.3 Alfas and more than a match for the Bugattis. Campari won the French Grand Prix in a 2·9 and Nuvolari, turning to Maserati after a disagreement with Enzo Ferrari, took first place from the latter's P.3s in the Belgian Grand Prix and at Nice and Montenero.

Whitney Straight brought the first 2·9s to England in 1934, installed a Wilson pre-selector gearbox in place of the normal unit and raced the cars successfully here, on the Continent and in South Africa. Later Bira was consistently successful with an ex-Whitney Straight car (one of the three 'British' 2·9s to reappear after the Second World War).

SPECIFICATION

Engine: 8 cylinders; 69 × 100 mm.; 2,992 c.c.; twin o.h.c.; Roots-type supercharger; max. power: 205 b.h.p. at 5,500 r.p.m. (68·5 b.h.p. per litre).

Frame: Channel.

Suspension: Front: rigid axle and semi-elliptics; rear: live axle and semi-elliptics. Friction shock absorbers.

Brakes: Hydraulic drum.

Dimensions: Wheelbase: 8 ft. 5½ in.; track, front and rear, 4 ft. 5 in.

32 *In his last Grand Prix car, the Type 59, Bugatti clung to the traditional layout—offset cockpit with transmission alongside the driver. (Benoist, 1934 French Grand Prix.)*

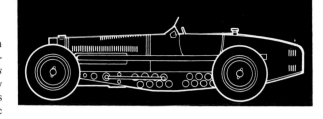

IN 1931 ETTORE BUGATTI replaced his historic Type 35 with the outwardly similar Type 51 (twin-o.h.c., 160 b.h.p. straight-eight), a moderately successful car which won three *grandes épreuves* and eight secondary G.P.s in that year, was the only car to beat the Alfas in 1932 (at Brno), and won three G.P.s in 1933. Attempts to regain his former pre-eminence with the 1931–32 Types 54 and 53 (a four-wheel drive car which never raced) flopped and he therefore spent 1933 building the Type 59—generally considered the last of a line of 'classic' Grand Prix cars stretching back to the Golden Age of Motor Racing.

In outline the engine followed Bugatti's earlier straight-eights (and was very closely related to the Type 57 sports car unit), but using plain instead of roller bearings and two valves per cylinder operated by twin o.h.c. driven from the rear. Power was transmitted through a separate gearbox to a double reduction final drive in the rear axle. Bugatti had, of necessity, used i.f.s. on the Type 53, but retreated again in the Type 59, conceding only a slight measure of independence by dividing the front beam axle at its centre. The spokes in the wheels were little more than reinforcement, a disc attached to the brake drum and the inner edge of the rim taking most of the stresses.

The 2·8-litre Type 59 ran in the last race of 1933 and the first of 1934, the Spanish G.P. (Varzi 4th, Dreyfus 6th) and the Monaco G.P. (Dreyfus 3rd, Nuvolari 5th). It first raced with a 3·3-litre engine in the French G.P., Benoist being fourth, flagged-off three laps behind the winner. Dreyfus and Brivio were first and second in the Belgian Grand Prix, Dreyfus second in the Swiss event and Nuvolari third in Spain. While British private owners had some success in 1935, the works cars appeared only spasmodically. Two last-ditch versions, a 3·8-litre and a 4·7-litre with a central cockpit, were never seriously developed and for the rest of his career Bugatti concentrated on sports cars.

SPECIFICATION

Engine: 8 cylinders; 72 × 100 mm.; 3,257 c.c.; twin o.h.c.; Roots-type supercharger; max. power: 240 b.h.p. at 5.400 r.p.m. (73·7 b.h.p. per litre).

Frame: Channel.

Suspension: Front: divided beam axle; and semi-elliptics; rear: live axle, reversed quarter-elliptics and radius arms. Friction shock absorbers.

Brakes: Mechanical drum.

Dimensions: Wheelbase: 8 ft. 6¼ in.; track, front and rear, 4 ft. 1¼ in.

34 *Although a rear-engined Grand Prix car was not a complete novelty, the P-Wagen was decidedly unconventional in 1934. (Hans Stuck enjoying the dubious honour of driving the last running German car in the 1934 French Grand Prix débâcle at Montlhéry.)*

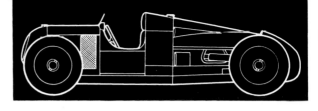

SPURRED ON BY Government backing in the intensely nationalistic atmosphere of the thirties, two German concerns prepared teams of radically new Grand Prix cars for the first season of racing under the 750-kg. Formula. The first of these to race was the spectacularly unconventional P-Wagen. Sponsored by a consortium of minor car manufacturers (Audi, D.K.W., Horch and Wanderer), the car was designed by Dr. Ferdinand Porsche, doubtless influenced in his choice of layout by his associate, Adolf Rosenberger, who had driven the first rear-engined G.P. car, the 1923 Benz Tropfwagen.

Porsche placed his V-16 engine between the driver and the rear axle, mounting it in a rigid tubular frame. All four wheels were independently sprung, by trailing arms and torsion bars at the front and a swing axle at the rear. The gearbox was mounted behind the rear axle, the drive being carried from the crankshaft under the differential and then forward again. On the assumption that weight distribution would remain unaltered as fuel was consumed if the latter were carried about the centre of gravity, the fuel tank was placed immediately behind the cockpit.

In practice, handling difficulties were a constant problem with the Auto Unions, for most drivers had to unlearn developed 'seat of the pants' faculties and adapt themselves to new techniques. The car's first race was at Avus; two of the team retired and the survivor finished third. The whole team retired when the P-Wagen first raced outside Germany (French G.P.). But, as drivers gained experience and the cars

reliability, the Auto Union team went on to win the 1934 German, Swiss and Czechoslovak Grands Prix.

In 1935, with its engine bored out to 4·95 litres and torsion bars replacing the rear transverse leaf spring, the car was redesignated the B-Type and was usually runner-up to its Stuttgart rival, winning only one *grande epreuve*, at Monza, and two secondary races from Mercedes.

SPECIFICATION

Engine: 16 cylinders (45° V-16); 68 × 75 mm.; 4,360 c.c.; single camshaft (between banks); Roots-type supercharger; max. power: 295 b.h.p. at 4,500 r.p.m. (67·7 b.h.p. per litre).

Frame: Tubular steel.

Suspension: Front: independent—trailing links and torsion bars; rear: swing axle and transverse leaf springs. Friction shock absorbers.

Brakes: Hydraulic drum.

Dimensions: Wheelbase: 9 ft. 2 in.; track, front and rear 4 ft. 8 in.

36 *First of a series of G.P. Mercedes-Benz that turned motor racing upside down in the thirties, the Type W.25. (Fagioli at Monaco, 1935.)*

MERCEDES-BENZ W.25

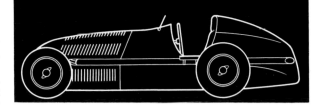

MERCEDES-BENZ DECIDED to return to Grand Prix racing in 1933, and by the beginning of the following year their design team, headed by Dr. Hans Nibel, had completed the first W.25. Although less unconventional than the P-Wagen, this was a very advanced car by contemporary standards. Independent front suspension; independent rear suspension; a gearbox/ differential unit attached to the frame, and therefore sprung weight, and hydraulic brakes were brought together for the first time in a 'conventional'—i.e. front-engined—racing car.

The M.25* engine, on the other hand, followed orthodox Mercedes-Benz practice in that individually-forged cylinders were held together by a welded-on water jacket. This unit had four valves per cylinder, twin overhead camshafts, a one-piece crankshaft and a Roots-type supercharger mounted in the nose feeding air to the two carburetters at an automatically-controlled rate. In its first 3·36-litre form (M.25A) it gave over 350 b.h.p., by the end of 1934 this had been increased by 40 b.h.p. in the 3·71-litre version, the 3·99-litre M.25B of 1935 produced 430 b.h.p. and in the basically-similar 1936 engine (4·74 litres) output was raised to 495 b.h.p.—thus Mercedes-Benz kept constantly several steps ahead of their non-German rivals in the power race which developed under the 750-kg. Formula.

The W.25 won only four races (two *grandes épreuves* and two secondary events) in 1934 and the Mercedes team experienced particularly galling defeats at Montlhéry and Berne. At the end of the season they shared with Auto Union Hitler's

* In Mercedes-Benz nomenclature the prefix W simply means Wagen, whilst M stands for Motor.

prize of £41,500 for the most successful German constructor. In 1935, however, they were beaten only four times, Caracciola winning the Eifelrennen and Belgian, French, Spanish, Swiss and Tripoli Grands Prix; Fagioli the Monaco, Peña Rhin and Avus events.

The 1936 car, which had its enlarged engine installed in a new short-wheelbase chassis, was far less successful, for after winning two early-season races it was consistently defeated—indeed, its showing was so poor that Mercedes-Benz withdrew their entries for three Italian races in the late summer.

SPECIFICATION

Engine (M.25B): 8 cylinders; 82 × 94·5 mm.; 3,990 c.c.; twin o.h.c.; Roots-type supercharger; max. power: 430 b.h.p. at 5,800 r.p.m. (107·8 b.h.p. per litre).
Frame: Box section.
Suspension: Front: independent—wishbones and coil springs; rear: independent—swing axle and transverse quarter-elliptics. Hydraulic shock absorbers.
Brakes: Hydraulic drum.
Dimensions: Wheelbase: 8 ft. 11 in.; track, front, 4 ft. 10 in., rear, 4 ft. 7 in.

38 *With the E.R.A. a British single-seater once again became a force on the Continent. (Grand Prix des Voiturettes, Dieppe, 1935: no. 10, Seaman in R.1B—1,500 c.c.; no. 4, Mays in R.4B—1,500 c.c.; no. 12, Fairfield in R.4A—1,100c.c. (winner); no. 8, Bira in R.2B 'Romulus'—1,500 c.c.)*

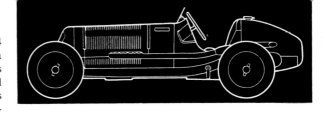

ENGLISH RACING AUTOMOBILES LTD. was founded in 1934 with the financial backing of Humphrey T. Cook to produce a developed single-seater version of Raymond Mays's famous 'White Riley' of 1933. The E.R.A., which in inspiration owed much to the Continental monopostos of the early thirties, was the work of three men—Peter Berthon, Reid Railton, responsible for the chassis, and T. Murray-Jamieson, the supercharger expert.

The engine was a perfectly straightforward pushrod o.h.v. 'six' of three alternative capacities—1,500 c.c.; 1,100 c.c. (shorter stroke) and 2 litres (increased bore and stroke). The A- and B-types used a Roots-type supercharger mounted vertically in front of the engine; the later cars had a Zoller unit (above the gearbox on the C-type, on the right of the engine in the E-type). Wilson pre-selective gearboxes were an unusual standard component on A, B and C cars.

The frame, too, was simple and slightly improved in successive models. Only the E-type had independent suspension, but several of the earlier cars were individually modified, e.g. fitted with Tecnauto i.f.s.

Between 1934 and 1936, seventeen cars were laid down, four A-types and the remainder basically B-types, several of which were later modified to 'C' specification. They became familiar on the circuits of Europe—winning many races, breaking class records and climbing hills very rapidly—upholding British prestige during an otherwise bleak period. Bira's 'Romulus' (R.2B), with ten firsts, eight seconds and five thirds gained from thirty starts in leading races, was the most successful car on the circuits; Mays's R.4B, which started life as the works test-bed and was progressively developed to become R.4D, was outstanding in British hill-climbs for many years, its competitive life continuing for some time after the war.

Lack of proper development hamstrung the E-type, and the solitary G-type, which had a Bristol engine and was related in little but name to the earlier cars, was a dismal failure. Many of the cars built in the mid-thirties are still active today. Immediately after the war they were more than mere grid-fillers and achieved honourable placings in several *grandes épreuves*.

SPECIFICATION (B-TYPE)

Engine: 6 cylinders; 57·5 × 95·2 mm.; 1,488 c.c.; pushrod o.h.v.; Roots-type supercharger; max. power: 150 b.h.p. at 6,500 r.p.m. (100·8 b.h.p. per litre).
Frame: Channel.
Suspension: Front: rigid axle and semi-elliptics; rear: live axle and semi-elliptics. Friction shock absorbers.
Brakes: Mechanical drum.
Dimensions: Wheelbase: 8 ft.; track, front, 4 ft. 4½ in., rear, 4 ft.

40 *The increased power of the 1936–37 Auto Union magnified its handling peculiarities and only Rosemeyer (seen here) really mastered the car. (Donington, 1937.)*

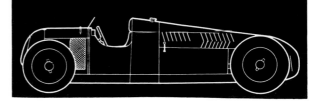

FERDINAND PORSCHE SOUGHT to get back on to even terms with Mercedes-Benz in 1936 primarily by further increasing the size of the Auto Union engine. The general design of the car remained unaltered, the extra space made available in the body by a slight extension of the wheelbase being used to house a larger fuel tank holding 46 gallons. Thereby, in effect, the driver was pushed a little farther away from the rear wheels, his difficulties apparently not appreciated until von Eberhorst, Werner and Feuereissen took over the Auto Union design from Dr. Porsche in 1937.

Without increasing its weight or dimensions the capacity of the V-16 engine was raised to 6,006 c.c. The compression ratio and r.p.m. were also raised, the output of 520 b.h.p. comparing favourably with the 494 b.h.p. given by the ME.25 Mercedes, but in terms of sheer power output the Auto Union team were at a considerable disadvantage against the W.125. The car weighed-in 'dry' (throughout the term of the Formula this meant minus not only fluids but also wheels and tyres) at 710 kg., well within the 750-kg. limit, but it actually came to the grid weighing over 950 kg.

Berndt Rosemeyer, who had served his motor-racing apprenticeship on the 1935 B-Type and by the following year was a top-flight driver, was the only man to fully exploit the car's potential. He won the German, Italian and Swiss Grands Prix, the Coppa Acerbo and the Eifelrennen (in thick fog and at a speed only 0·3 m.p.h. lower than the previous year's record). Varzi scored Auto Union's sixth win of the season at Tripoli and the team lost only five races, two to Mercedes and three to the combination of Nuvolari and Alfa Romeo.

With the W.125, Mercedes regained the ascendancy in 1937, winning seven races against Auto Union, who also lost one minor event, in Rio de Janeiro, to Alfa Romeo. Hasse won at Spa and von Delius in South Africa, but Auto Union increasingly depended on Rosemeyer, who won the Eifelrennen, Coppa Acerbo, Vanderbilt Cup and the last race run under the 750 kg. Formula, the Donington Grand Prix.

SPECIFICATION

Engine: 16 cylinders (45° V-16); 75 × 85 mm.; 6,006 c.c.; single camshaft (between banks); Roots-type supercharger; max. power: 520 b.h.p. at 5,000 r.p.m. 86·6 b.h.p. per litre).

Frame: Tubular.

Suspension: Front: independent—trailing links and torsion bars; rear: independent—swing axle and torsion bars. Friction shock absorbers.

Brakes: Hydraulic drum.

Dimensions: Wheelbase: 9 ft. 6½ in.; track, front and rear, 4 ft. 8 in.

Most powerful Grand Prix car ever built, the Mercedes-Benz W.125 dominated its only season of racing—even though its drivers were seldom able to make full use of its 646 b.h.p. (Lang, Freiburg.)

MERCEDES-BENZ W.125

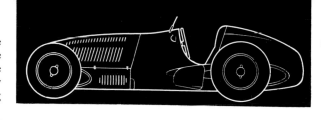

BY MERCEDES-BENZ standards the 1936 W.25E was a failure and they therefore built an entirely new car, the W.125, for the last season of the 750-kg. Formula. This proved to be the most powerful Grand Prix car ever built and was theoretically capable of exceeding 200 m.p.h., speeds little below this being timed on the Spa circuit.

The chassis was actually designed to take a 3·5-litre engine for races under a formula which was due to come into effect in 1937, but which was postponed for twelve months and subsequently modified. It was built around two large and extremely rigid tubular side members. Enclosed coil springs were abandoned in the i.f.s. layout and a de Dion axle was used at the rear for the first time in a road-racing car. This eliminated the natural oversteer of the W.25, thus giving the driver a greater degree of control (with over 600 b.h.p. at his disposal he could always induce oversteer when necessary). Into the chassis a 5·66-litre engine—the ultimate development of the M.25, bored-out to 94 mm. and still giving its maximum output at 5,800 r.p.m.—was fitted. The supercharger was no longer used to blow pure air, Mercedes at last conforming to normal practice and installing it between the carburetters and the cylinders (and gaining a substantial bonus in terms of b.h.p.). Although the power unit was 45 lb. heavier than the M.25, the 'dry' weight of the car was kept within the 750-kg. maximum. Outwardly, the body lines followed those of the W.25 and a fully-streamlined version was produced for Avus.

Mercedes-Benz convincingly re-established their Grand Prix superiority with the W.125, winning seven races to Auto Union's five in 1937, all other marques being eclipsed. Their leading driver, Rudolf Caracciola, won the German, Swiss, Italian and Czechoslovak Grands Prix; Hermann Lang won at Avus and Tripoli; von Brauchitsch at Monaco. A newcomer to the team, Dick Seaman, was second in the Vanderbilt Cup, fourth in the Italian and Masaryk G.P.s and fifth in the Avusrennen and Coppa Acerbo.

SPECIFICATION

Engine: 8 cylinders; 94 × 102 mm.; 5,660 c.c.; twin o.h.c.; Roots-type supercharger; max. power: 646 b.h.p. at 5,800 r.p.m. (114·1 b.h.p. per litre).

Frame: Oval and round tubes.

Suspension: Front: independent—wishbones and coil springs; rear: de Dion axle, torsion bars and radius rods. Hydraulic shock absorbers.

Brakes: Hydraulic drum.

Dimensions: Wheelbase: 9 ft. 2 in.; track, front, 4 ft. 10 in.; rear, 4 ft. 7 in.

44 *Peak of development of the pre-war Austin single-seaters was reached in the o.h.v. 750, which had classic—if fore-shortened—G.P. car lines. (Hadley, 1938 Coronation Trophy, Donington.)*

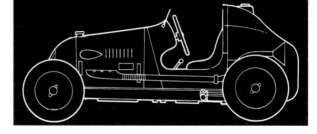

LAST OF A long line of pre-war Austin racing cars related to the famous Seven, the o.h.c. 750s of 1936–39 were also the last monopostos built, maintained and raced as a team by a major British car manufacturer. In various guises and tuned to varying degrees, Sevens were raced by private owners and by factory teams—Herbert Austin valued racing experience in developing production cars—from the early twenties until 1939.

The pure racing Sevens gradually grew away from their bread and butter relations and the last firm link was broken in 1936, when the side-valve engine was at last abandoned in favour of a 744-c.c. o.h.c. unit. This was designed by T. Murray Jamieson and, from the outset, his intention was to build an engine suitable for extended development. The aim was to eventually peak at 12,000 r.p.m., although during its active career it was scarcely taken above 9,000 and then only in sprints. The supercharger, gear-driven from the crankshaft, was mounted behind the engine and the transmission was dropped (through a double-reduction drive) to 4 in. below the rear axle centre to reduce cockpit height. The simple chassis and suspension followed, at least superficially, the usual Austin Seven practice.

Of the three cars built, one was sent to Germany and all suffered teething troubles in their first season. In 1937 and 1938, however, the two works cars went from success to success in British races and hill-climbs, Charles Dodson's first place in the 1938 Empire Trophy setting the seal on an outstanding season. Only one car was run in 1939 and the last victory came in the Imperial Trophy race at Crystal Palace in August of that year. During their career the o.h.c. Austins also took nineteen international class records and some indication of their ultimate potential can be gained from Dodson's all-time class lap record of 121·2 m.p.h. for the Brooklands outer circuit (the out-and-out record—143·44 m.p.h.—standing to Cobb's Napier-Railton).

SPECIFICATION

Engine: 4 cylinders; 60 × 65 mm.; 744 c.c.; twin o.h.c.; Jamieson Roots-type supercharger; max. power: 98 b.h.p. at 7,800 r.p.m.—116 b.h.p. on 'sprint' fuel (131·7 b.h.p. per litre).

Frame: Channel.

Suspension: Front: rigid axle and transverse spring; rear: live axle and quarter elliptics. Friction shock absorbers.

Brakes: Cable-operated drum.

Dimensions: Wheelbase: 6 ft. 10 in.; track, front and rear, 3 ft. 11 in.

46 *Unmistakably a Maserati, but rarely seen in Europe, the 8CTF had a remarkable record, under various names, in American racing. (Villoresi, Donington, 1938.)*

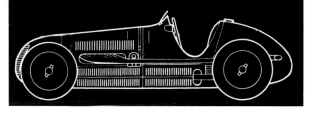

DESPITE THEIR PREOCCUPATION with 1·5-litre cars, Alfa Romeo and Maserati continued to support the Grand Prix Formula in 1938 and 1939. Maserati's 3-litre car, the 8C, was almost obsolescent in Europe, but it was advanced by American standards and rudely upset the established order at Indianapolis in 1939.

In general the car's welded box-section chassis conformed to standard Maserati practice (the 'X' bracing at the rear serving as an oil tank/cooler) and the engine resembled their four-cylinder 1·5-litre units (cast-iron cylinders in blocks of four, front-mounted superchargers gear-driven from the crankshaft, as were the camshafts). The 8CL engine had a slightly larger bore and reduced stroke (78 × 78 mm.) and thirty-two valves in place of sixteen—in effect a 'doubled' version of the 4CL 1·5-litre with a claimed output of 420 b.h.p.

In European races the two works 8CTFs were fast during the opening laps, more than once leading the German cars before retiring, overstressed. Trossi kept one motoring for the duration of the 1938 Italian G.P., finishing fifth, and in the cars' last 'works' outing, the 1939 German G.P., Pietsch finished third, a lap down on Caracciola. Taken over by Laury Schell, the cars ran once more in Europe in the 1939 Swiss G.P. (Dreyfus 8th).

In 1939 Wilbur Shaw firmly reinstated the supercharged multi-cylinder as a force at Indianapolis, winning in the new Boyle Special 8CTF at 115.035 m.p.h. All the 8Cs then built, three 8CTFs and one 8CL, ran in the 1940 '500'. Shaw won

again, Dreyfus and LeBegue finished tenth in one of the Schell cars and Riganti crashed his 8CL. Trying for a hat-trick in 1941, Shaw crashed when leading in the Boyle 8CTF. Ted Horn was third in this car in 1946 and 1947, and fourth in 1948. Villoresi finished seventh in one of the two new 8CLs in the 1946 race. Before retiring Lee Wallard several times led the 1949 '500' in an 8C and although age was now beginning to tell, this car ran again in 1950. The splendid Indianapolis career of the 8C Maseratis ended when the Auto Accessories Special crashed during the 1951 qualifying trials.

SPECIFICATION

Engine: 8 cylinders; 69 × 100 mm.; 2,990 c.c.; twin o.h.c.; two Roots-type superchargers; max. power: 355 b.h.p. at 6,500 r.p.m. (118·7 b.h.p. per litre).

Frame: Channel.

Suspension: Front: independent—wishbones and torsion bars; rear: live axle and quarter-elliptics. Hydraulic shock absorbers.

Brakes: Hydraulic drum.

Dimensions: Wheelbase: 9 ft. (approx.)

48 *Brauchitsch holds the W.163 in a full-blooded drift.*
Although much less powerful than the W.125, it was
no slower round the circuits. (Rheims, 1939.)

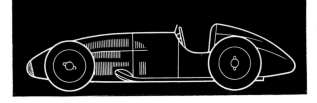

EARLY IN 1937 Mercedes-Benz started work on a new 2·96-litre V-12 engine, dropping their eight-in-line arrangement in a search for more power per litre under regulations which limited supercharged engine capacity to 3 litres and raised the minimum weight limit to 850 kg.

The M.154 used in the W.154 and W.163 inherited detail features from its predecessors, but the relative piston area and r.p.m. were increased and two in-series superchargers fed it with mixture under high, instead of low, pressure. In 1939 it was producing over 480 b.h.p. compared with the 645 given by the M.125, the drop in power being held to just over 150 b.h.p. when 1,698 c.c. were 'lost'.

To compensate for this loss of power and for the obligatory increase in weight, an efficient body and good roadholding qualities were prerequisites. The engine was mounted at an angle to the centre-line and canted down towards the rear, whence the transmission passed alongside the cockpit. The low overall height achieved was not accompanied by a noticeable reduction in frontal area, as the width of the body was increased, but this in turn contributed to stability and consequently to roadholding, thus more of the available power could be used on more of the circuit. The chassis, taken from the W.125, was common to both the W.154 and W.163, but the latter had a smoother body, notably around the nose with its uncharacteristic narrow grille.

This combination of power and efficiency was almost all-conquering in 1939, the W.163 being beaten only twice by the Auto Union D-Type. One car turned up at Indianapolis in 1947 and climbed to fourth before retiring; in 1948 its complexities defeated the American crew. Then in 1951 Mercedes-Benz sent a team of three W.163s to run in the Argentine *Formule Libre* races. Still not quite *au point*, even in the hands of Unterturkheim mechanics, and handicapped on the twisting Palermo Park circuit at Buenos Aires, they finished second and third to Gonzales's 2-litre Ferrari in two races.

SPECIFICATION

Engine: 12 cylinders (60° V-12); 67 × 70 mm.; 2,962 c.c.; four o.h.c.; two Roots-type superchargers; max. power: 483 b.h.p. at 7,800 r.p.m. (163·1 b.h.p. per litre).

Frame: Tubular.

Suspension: Front: independent—wishbones and coil springs; rear: de Dion axle and torsion bars. Hydraulic shock absorbers.

Brakes: Hydraulic drum.

Dimensions: Wheelbase: 8 ft. 11 in.; track, front, 4 ft. 10 in., rear, 4 ft. 7 in.

50 *The virtually unbeatable Type 158 Alfa Romeo began life as a voiturette and reigned supreme in the post-war Grands Prix. (Fangio, who won his first World Championship with these cars in 1951, at Silverstone in 1950.)*

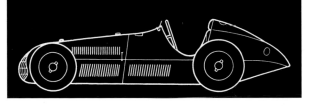

SEEING LITTLE PROSPECT of breaking the German grip on Grand Prix racing, Italian constructors increasingly concentrated on the 1·5-litre class in the late thirties, aided and abetted by their national Federation, which confined Italian races to this capacity in 1939, and encouraged by the prospect of a 1·5-litre Grand Prix Formula taking effect in 1941. Alfa Romeo's entry in this class was the Type 158, progenitor of one of the most successful Grand Prix cars ever built.

Colombo virtually built the 158 around one bank of cylinders from his V-16. The resultant straight-eight (the twin o.h.c., supercharger and auxiliaries gear-driven from the front) initially gave just under 200 b.h.p. Driving through a gearbox differential unit, it was installed in a tubular chassis. These 'Alfettas' fulfilled their 1938 promise in 1939, being beaten only once (by Mercedes at Tripoli).

The cars survived the war, reappearing in the *Formule Libre* races of 1946 and automatically becoming Grand Prix cars under the new Formula in 1947. Two-stage supercharging raised output to 250 b.h.p. This was further increased to 265, still at 7,500 r.p.m., in the 158/47 raced in 1948. The twelve-year-old design was then revitalized as the Type 159 in 1950, a de Dion axle being used at the rear, whilst an increase in engine speed to 8,500 r.p.m. and detailed improvements produced 350 b.h.p. (at some cost in reliability as the associated stresses became manifest). The final version, the 1951 Type 159A, had further developed brakes and increased tankage (consumption had by then dropped below 2 m.p.g.).

This progressive development paid enormous dividends, the cars overwhelming their opposition in the *grandes épreuves* of 1947–48 and 1950 (Alfa Romeo did not race in 1949), gaining thirty-one victories in thirty-five starts between 1947 and their final withdrawal in 1951. They first appeared in Britain in 1950, Farina, Fagioli and Parnell finishing 1, 2, 3 in the G.P. d'Europe at Silverstone, the circuit where they were first defeated by the 4·5-litre Ferrari in the following year. They came back to win their last race, the 1951 Spanish G.P.

SPECIFICATION (TYPE 159A)

Engine: 8 cylinders; 58 × 70 mm.; 1,479 c.c.; twin o.h.c.; two Roots-type superchargers; max. power: 385 b.h.p. at 9,500 r.p.m. (260·3 b.h.p. per litre).

Frame: Tubular.

Suspension: Front: independent—trailing arms and transverse leaf spring; rear: de Dion axle and radius rods. Telescopic shock absorbers.

Brakes: Hydraulic drum.

Dimensions: Wheelbase: 8 ft. 2 in.; track, front and rear, 4 ft. 1 in.

52 *The 4CL Maserati became almost as popular with independent drivers in the late forties as the Type 35 Bugatti
had been twenty years earlier. (Bira in the 1949 British
Grand Prix which de Graffenried won with a similar car.)*

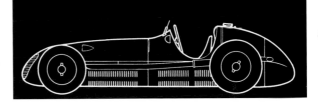

RACED ONLY SPASMODICALLY by the works, the 1·5-litre four-cylinder Maseratis of 1946–51 were one of the mainstays of the independent teams and it was not uncommon to see nine or ten of these cars in a major Grand Prix.

The 4CL first appeared (at Brooklands) in 1939, its 'square' —78 × 78 mm.—engine having four valves per cylinder and, with a single-stage Roots blower, giving 210 b.h.p. Unusual features of the car were an oil tank forming a massive chassis cross-member under the cockpit, front springing by long parallel torsion bars and a steering-box behind the engine operating two separate linkages to the front wheels. The 4CLT, introduced in 1947, differed chiefly in having a tubular instead of channel-section frame, and with two-stage super-charging the power was about 225 b.h.p. When the Maserati brothers left to form O.S.C.A. the lower, coil-sprung 4CLT/48 was developed under Signor Orsi's direction. Two-stage super-charging was made standard and the engine itself was sub-stantially re-designed, now producing 240 b.h.p.

The 4CL raced briefly, and promisingly, before the war, but the developed post-war versions never matched the Alfa Romeos. The 4CLT/48 first appeared in June 1948 and was first and second in its first race, at San Remo, a name by which it was thus often known. Other successes followed—Fangio won his first European race with a Scuderia Achille Varzi car at San Remo in 1949—but Alfa Romeo's withdrawal from racing did not leave the Maseratis completely in command. Attempts to gain more power from an eleven-year-old engine,

mainly by raising supercharger pressures, drastically reduced reliability and retirements—the drivers oil-soaked—became increasingly common.

A few independents, notably Speluzzi of Scuderia Milan and Enrico Platé, gave the cars more power (as much as 275 b.h.p. was claimed) to try to keep them competitive in 1950–51, but with little reward. Even the long-stroke (1,720 c.c.) models built for the 1950 Argentine Temporada and giving nearly 290 b.h.p. were just not fast enough.

SPECIFICATION (4CLT/48)

Engine: 4 cylinders; 78 × 78 mm.; 1,498 c.c.; twin o.h.c.; Roots-type supercharger; max. power: 240 b.h.p. at 7,000 r.p.m. (160·2 b.h.p. per litre).
Frame: Tubular.
Suspension: Front: independent—coil springs and wishbones; rear: live axle and quarter-elliptics. Hydraulic shock absorbers.
Brakes: Hydraulic drum.
Dimensions: Wheelbase: 8 ft. 2½ in.; track, front, 3 ft. 11½ in., rear, 4 ft. 1½ in.

54 *For the first post-war Formula 1, France could field several drivers of Grand Prix calibre, but her only cars, the 4·5-litre Talbots were seldom more than place-fillers. (Rear wheels spinning, Etancelin accelerates out of Thillois, Rheims, 1948.)*

IN THE OPENING years of the first post-war Formula 1 only Talbot eschewed the power potential—and high associated stresses—of supercharging, using instead a 4·5-litre unblown engine developed from their 1938–39 4-litre single-cam unit (a modified 1939 single-cam car was, in fact, driven by Louis Chiron between 1945 and 1948).

The engine of Anthony Lago's 1948 Talbot was a long-stroke six-cylinder with a camshaft on each side of the block operating short pushrods to the overhead valves. An epicyclic preselector gearbox drove through spur gears which offset the transmission to the right, the driver, who sat very low, using the padded propeller-shaft tunnel as an armrest. Essentially 'old-fashioned', with a leaf-sprung live rear axle, the car's only notable feature was an elaborate oil-cooler across the scuttle.

Although nearly 2 cwt. heavier and 60 b.h.p. less powerful than the dominant Alfa Romeo 158, the Talbot ran more economically (8–9 m.p.g. against 2–4 m.p.g.) and so could complete a regulation 500 km. *grande épreuve* with, at most, one stop for fuel against the two or three of the blown 1·5-litre cars. Hare-and-tortoise tactics thus allowed the outclassed Talbots to cause even Alfa drivers to overstress their engines on occasions, and when the Italian team withdrew for a season (1949) the Talbots showed an ability to beat the less reliable Maseratis and early Ferraris, winning the Paris and Belgian Grands Prix and the Rheims 'Grand Prix de France', and finishing second in the Czech, Italian and Marseilles Grands Prix.

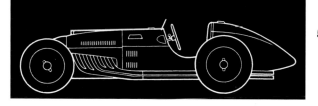

In 1950 an improved Talbot appeared, with *inter alia* two plugs per cylinder (used experimentally in 1949) and three horizontal instead of downdraught carburetters; power was increased from around 240 to 275 b.h.p.; a bigger fuel tank was fitted and cable brakes gave way to hydraulic. These cars were faster, but so was the opposition, and although they won occasionally they remained primarily the reliable place-fillers of previous years. Then, late in 1950, the 4·5-litre unblown Ferrari appeared and beat M. Lago at his own game.

SPECIFICATION

Engine: 6 cylinders; 93 × 110 mm.; 4,485 c.c.; pushrod o.h.v.; max. power: 275 b.h.p. at 5,000 r.p.m. (61.3 b.h.p. per litre).

Frame: Channel.

Suspension: Front: independent—wishbones and transverse leaf spring; rear: live axle and semi-elliptics. Hydraulic and friction shock absorbers.

Brakes: Hydraulic drum.

Dimensions: Wheelbase: 8 ft. 2½ in.; track, front, 4 ft. 6 in., rear, 4 ft. 3½ in.

56 *By the mid-fifties, the Cooper 500 was a sophisticated machine, as well as being remarkably effective, with which drivers fought out close and entertaining battles on circuits all over the world. (J. Russell, Brands Hatch, 1954.)*

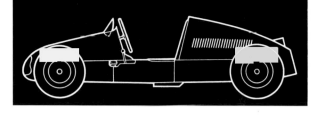

THE COOPER 500 uniquely transformed half-litre competition from a thinly-supported amateur class into an International Formula, dominated it for over ten years and, in so doing, killed it through lack of opposition. Built by the hundred, the car also won races in similar quantity.

The prototype was built in June 1946 by Charles Cooper—one time tuner of Kaye Don's racing cars—his son John, and Eric Brandon, who was to have a second car. Into a box-section and tubular frame were fitted chassis units from the Fiat 500 coupé, there being two wishbone and transverse leaf-spring front suspension assemblies, one at each end. Mounted behind the driver were a J.A.P. single-cylinder o.h.c. motorcycle speedway engine and Triumph gearbox driving the rear axle by chain.

First appearances, at Prescott hill-climbs, showed that 40–45 b.h.p. was too much for the engine bearers, but flexible mounting overcame this and the car began winning sprint events impressively. For 1948 twelve lighter, slimmer cars were laid down, with cast Elektron wheels in place of Fiat discs, and circuit racing began. With over 150 b.h.p./ton these nimble machines gave such drivers as Stirling Moss—who won eleven of his first fifteen events—a valuable introduction to monoposto racing. Large-scale production began at the end of 1948 and 500 c.c. championships thereafter fell to Cooper with monotonous regularity. In 1950, 500-c.c. racing became the F.I.A. Formula 3.

Developed year by year—the Marks reached XI by 1957—the Cooper 500 assumed such refinements as rack and pinion steering (Mk. V, 1951); all-tubular chassis (Mk. VI, 1952); slimmer body with scuttle fuel tank (Mk. VIII, 1954) and disc rear brakes (Mk. IX, 1955). Although the J.A.P. engine remained standard for a long time, the major development was the widespread adoption of the considerably more expensive and potent twin-o.h.c. Norton engine in 1950–51.

By the end of the fifties, virtually one-make (Cooper) racing had lost its appeal, but the little Cooper had meanwhile fathered a line of larger cars. . . .

SPECIFICATION (MK. X, XI)

Engine (Norton): 1 cylinder; 86 × 86·5 mm.; 499 c.c.; twin o.h.c.; max. power: 48 b.h.p. at 7,200 r.p.m. (96·2 b.h.p. per litre).

Frame: Tubular.

Suspension: Front: independent—wishbones and transverse leaf spring; rear: independent—wishbones and transverse leaf spring.

Brakes: Hydraulic, drum front, disc rear.

Dimensions: Wheelbase: 7 ft. 3 in.; track, front, 3 ft. 9 in., rear, 3 ft. 7 in.

58 *The V-16 B.R.M. was an advanced and fantastically powerful design, but was never an effective contender under the Grand Prix Formula to which it was built. (Wharton, Goodwood, Easter 1954.)*

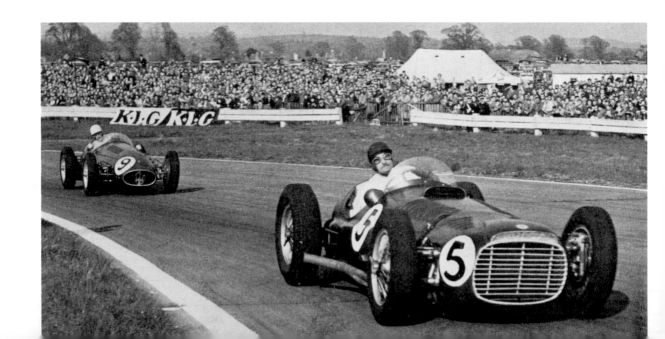

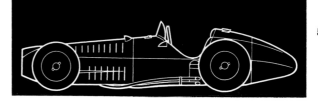

BY ALL REASONABLE counts the V-16 B.R.M. should have been the outstanding car of the first post-war Grand Prix Formula. Instead the initials became almost invariably associated with failure. . . .

The roots of the project reached back to 1939, when the old E.R.A. concern ceased operations, and to the continued determination of Raymond Mays and Peter Berthon to build an all-British Grand Prix winner. The co-operation of over 150 British firms was secured, design began in 1946, and the car was eventually unveiled late in 1949, proving to be a machine of fantastic technical complexity. The decision to use supercharging limited engine capacity to 1·5 litres and to obtain the maximum piston area a sixteen-cylinder layout was chosen. A ten-main-bearing crankshaft was used, the main output shaft below it driving the Rolls-Royce-designed supercharger at the front and transmitting power to a rear axle-mounted five-speed gearbox. Even using this fully, drivers found it difficult to keep r.p.m. within the restricted effective range (9–12,000). The frame was conventional but oleo-pneumatic struts (instead of torsion bars) were incorporated in the suspension of a racing car for the first time.

The car's first race appearance was in the 1950 International Trophy at Silverstone. The field left it on the line with a sheared drive-shaft, this débâcle hinting that the team's mechanical—and organizational—troubles were far from overcome. Their best *grande épreuve* performance came in the 1951 British Grand Prix on the same circuit, Parnell and Walker taking fifth and seventh places after heroic drives in seriously overheated cockpits. Thereafter, its original clean body marred by supplementary air intakes and louvres, and with its 'sprint-distance' reliability found, it was relegated to lesser *Formule Libre* events.

The scream of sixteen tiny cylinders—the one feature of the car which enthusiasts agreed was satisfactory—was heard in a race for the last time at Castle Combe in October 1955.

SPECIFICATION

Engine: 16 cylinders (135° V-16); 49·5 × 48·2 mm.; 1,488 c.c.; four o.h.c.; two-stage centrifugal supercharger; max. power: 475 b.h.p. at 11,500 r.p.m. (319 b.h.p. per litre).

Frame: Tubular.

Suspension: Front: independent—trailing arms and oleo-pneumatic struts; rear: de Dion axle and oleo-pneumatic struts.

Brakes: Hydraulic disc.

Dimensions: Wheelbase: 8 ft. 2 in.; track, front, 4 ft. 4 in., rear, 4 ft. 3 in.

60 *Although it appeared slightly ponderous from some angles, the 4·5 litre Ferrari was, in fact, very compact. (Gonzales, 1951 British Grand Prix, Silverstone.)*

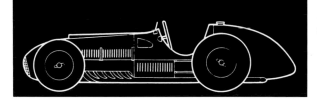

THE FIRST GRAND PRIX Ferrari, the 1·5-litre supercharged Type 125, appeared in 1948 and enjoyed some success against second-class opposition, but was no match for the Alfa Romeos. Ferrari therefore turned to the alternative offered by the Formula and at Spa in 1950 his first unsupercharged G.P. car, an interim 3·3-litre model, appeared. From this, through a 4·1-litre version, was developed the 4·5-litre V-12 which in 1951 broke the Alfa Romeo stranglehold on Grand Prix racing.

The design and development of the new engine was the first task of Aurelio Lampredi when he joined Ferrari in 1949. Basically it owed much to the Colombo-designed single-cam engines and like them was 'over-square'. A 60-degree V-12, it had one chain-driven o.h.c. for each bank and two valves (and from 1951 two plugs) per cylinder. The crankcase was split on the centre-line of the seven-bearing crankshaft and also formed the water jacket. This engine was set well back in the chassis with the gearbox behind and partly beneath the cockpit.

In its first race, the 1950 Italian G.P., the Ferrari demonstrated that 4·5 unsupercharged litres might, after all, match 1·5 blown litres, for Ascari's 4·5 finished second, only one minute behind Farina's Alfa. The 159As held their own in the first of the fierce inter-marque battles of 1951, then Gonzales beat them fairly and squarely in the British G.P. at Silverstone. The Ferrari also won the German and Italian G.P.s, the Alfas beating them only at Bari and Barcelona in the last half of the season. Thereafter the 4·5s were raced only occasionally by the factory, their 'works' career fizzling out at Albi in 1953. Tony Vandervell's 'Thinwall Special' version, however, became familiar on British circuits, fighting-out many 'sprint' events with the V-16 B.R.M.s.

With new chassis, lengthened wheelbase, wider track and engines developed to give 430 b.h.p., five new cars were built in 1952 and 1953 for the Indianapolis '500', but although Ascari managed to qualify one at 134·3 m.p.h. they made little impression in the American classic.

SPECIFICATION

Engine:　12 cylinders (60° V-12); 80 × 74·5 mm.; 4,498 c.c.; two o.h.c.; max. power: 380 b.h.p. at 7,000 r.p.m. (84·5 b.h.p. per litre).

Frame:　Tubular.

Suspension:　Front: independent—wishbones and transverse leaf springs; rear: de Dion axle and radius arms. Hydraulic shock absorbers.

Brakes:　Hydraulic drum.

Dimensions:　Wheelbase: 7 ft. 8 in.; track, front, 4 ft. 3½ in., rear, 4 ft. 3 in.

62 *Thoroughly conventional and never quite potent enough to really challenge the best Continental marques, the works H.W.M.s formed the first full British team to venture whole-heartedly into Grand Prix racing for many years. (Collins, Rouen, 1952.)*

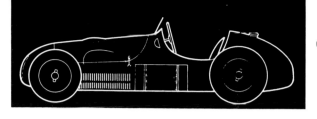

DURING 1950–53 ONLY one British marque, H.W.M., ran a continuous programme as a works team, mainly abroad, and successfully enough, at least in their first season, to show a profit. When, in 1952, potent Continental makes (and Connaught and Cooper-Bristol) concentrated on Formula 2 the H.W.M.s became outclassed and by 1954 faded away. However, for three years they earned remarkable prestige as well as regular place-money and, not least, gave such drivers as Stirling Moss and Peter Collins a foothold in international racing.

The H.W.M.s were designed and run (and sometimes driven) by John Heath and George Abecassis, who built them in their Hersham and Walton Motors workshops—hence H.W.M. Heath's success with a prototype, the 1949 two-seat H.W.-Alta, led to three cars being built for 1950. These had 'two-seat' bodies, but ran only in monoposto events, with success, and from them a true F.2 single-seater was derived, five being built for 1951. Like their predecessors, these used Geoffrey Taylor's 2-litre, four-cylinder, twin-o.h.c. engine and a Wilson/Armstrong Siddeley preselector gearbox with no clutch. Unlike the transverse-leaf-sprung 1950 models, they had a de Dion axle and quarter-elliptic rear springs, and coil-and-wishbone front suspension; 1952–53 cars had torsion-bar rear springing and inboard brakes.

The Alta engine gave 130 b.h.p. in 1951. Subsequent development (by 1953 little but the cylinder block remained original) brought increased power—but outstripped relia-bility. A braced twin-tube chassis carried light tubular body framing and the pre-1953 cars were high-built despite a low transmission line. Three lower, shorter, more powerful cars with Jaguar synchromesh gearboxes were built for 1953, but suffered continual troubles.

Best remembered for a 1–2 victory in the 1952 International Trophy at Silverstone and for the novice Moss's rousing chases of works Ferraris on the Continent, the H.W.M. won acclaim more for sustained professional competition on a small budget than for individual triumphs.

SPECIFICATION

Engine: 4 cylinders; 83·5 × 90 mm.; 1,960 c.c.; twin o.h.c.; max. power: 150 b.h.p. at 6,000 r.p.m. (76·5 b.h.p. per litre).

Frame: Tubular.

Suspension: Front: independent—coil springs and wishbones; rear: de Dion axle and torsion bars. Hydraulic shock absorbers.

Brakes: Hydraulic drum (inboard at rear).

Dimensions: Wheelbase: 7 ft. 9½ in.; track, front and rear, 4 ft. 1 in.

64 *From the small, neat grille, the Gordini's bonnet sloped up sharply to the scuttle, the high position of the cockpit above the transmission spoiling the otherwise small frontal area. (Behra, 1952 Belgian Grand Prix, Spa.)*

GORDINI 2-litre

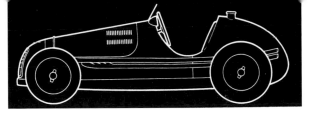

THE LAST FRENCH racing car to win a full international Grand Prix grew, in effect, out of the 1,100-c.c. Simca-Gordini voiturettes of 1947. By 1950 Amedée Gordini had developed a 1·5-litre car and into the frame of this he fitted a new 'square' six-cylinder 2-litre engine for the 1952 Formula 2 season, shedding his Simca connections in the process.

Features of this car were the straight tubular frame members and the unconventional suspension. Single arms, unbraced by triangulated members, were used in the i.f.s., and at the rear Gordini used a live axle (his reluctance to adopt a more contemporary—de Dion or swing-axle—arrangement resulted in poor handling qualities and caused transmission failures). He depended on light weight to compensate for lack of sheer engine power, his cars appearing delicate beside the dominant machine of 1952, the sturdy Ferrari.

Their appearance proved to be a true guide to their nature, but despite frailty of engine, transmission and suspension they offered the only serious challenge to the Ferrari team until the closing races of 1952. Their moment of triumph came in the fourth of the 1952 Grands Prix de France at Rheims, when Behra led from start to finish, his car not only being fast but, for once, reliable for the duration of a three-hour race. Driven by Behra, Manzon, Schell and Trintignant, Gordinis were second in two G.P.s (Cadours, Marseilles); third in four (Belgian, Comminges, Pau and Swiss); fourth at Rouen; fifth at the Nürburgring and Zandvoort.

For income to hold his *équipe* together, Gordini again had to race wherever possible in 1953, but lacked the resources to develop, or even adequately maintain, his cars between races. Inevitably Gordini retirements were common, successes rare (two minor wins, Cadours G.P. and Frontières G.P.), although Trintignant more than once briefly challenged the Italians.

With 2·5-litre engines the same cars carried the blue of France in 1954, but eventually even Amedée Gordini faltered, and after a final fling with a new car using an eight-cylinder version of the same engine he quietly withdrew from racing in 1957.

SPECIFICATION

Engine: 6 cylinders; 75 × 75 mm.; 1,960 c.c.; twin o.h.c.; max. power: 155 b.h.p. at 6,000 r.p.m. (79·1 b.h.p. per litre).
Frame: Tubular.
Suspension: Front: independent—transverse arms and torsion bars; rear: live axle and torsion bars. Hydraulic shock absorbers.
Brakes: Hydraulic drum.
Dimensions: Wheelbase: 7 ft. 6 in.; track, front and rear, 4 ft. 7 in.

66 *The well-proportioned body of the Type 500 precisely complemented the sound mechanical features of the car. (Ascari, Silverstone, 1953.)*

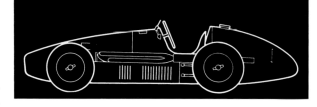

INTELLIGENT ANTICIPATION IN 1951—as in 1960—gave Ferrari mastery of the following season's *grandes épreuves*, each time with cars which differed fundamentally in design from their G.P. predecessors.

In 1951 the twelve-cylinder engine was set aside in favour of a Lampredi-designed 'four', which was installed in a shortened and lightened version of the 1950 V-12 chassis. The engine had a deep light-alloy crankcase containing the five-bearing crankshaft, from the front of which gear-trains drove the auxiliaries. Considerable attention was paid to the design of the exhaust and cooling systems—much of the cooling derived from alcohol was sacrificed, for, in order to give the car Grand Prix endurance without resort to enormous tanks, a low (20 per cent) alcohol-content fuel mixture was used. This engine proved outstandingly reliable, failing the team only once (at Syracuse in 1953). It was set well back in the chassis, the radiator was ahead of the front wheels and the transmission passed under the cockpit to the gearbox.

Apart from the incident at Syracuse, the Ferrari team was beaten once in 1952 (by Gordini) and once in 1953 (by Maserati), and Ascari gained two successive World Championships with the Type 500. Except at Rheims the cars were not really under pressure until the end of the 1952 season, when, at Monza, the A6G Maserati showed its potential and forecast its 1953 challenge.

Winter work on the Type 500 was confined to the engine and the two Italian teams started the season on fairly equal terms, the superior speed advantage of the Maserati cancelled out by the roadholding and reliability of the Ferrari. In the season's closest race, the French Grand Prix, Mike Hawthorn won his first championship event from Fangio's Maserati, by only 1·4 seconds. But the Ferrari team staved off outright defeat until the last race appearance of the works Type 500s (in the Italian Grand Prix), when Fangio won by less than two seconds.

SPECIFICATION

Engine: 4 cylinders; 90 × 78 mm.; 1,985 c.c.; twin o.h.c.; max. power: 180 b.h.p. at 7,200 r.p.m. (90·7 b.h.p. per litre).

Frame: Tubular.

Suspension: Front: independent—double wishbones and transverse springs; rear: de Dion axle, transverse leaf spring and radius rods. Hydraulic shock absorbers.

Brakes: Hydraulic drum.

Dimensions: Wheelbase: 7 ft. 2 in.; track, front, 4 ft. 3 in., rear, 4 ft. 1 in.

68 *The 250F Maserati had a longer front-line life than any other car built to the 1954–60 Formula and, despite its reputation for tricky handling, was very popular with independent drivers. (Behra, 1955 British Grand Prix, Aintree.)*

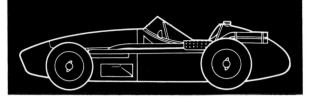

MAINSTAY OF THE independents during the first years of the 2·5-litre Formula and the car on which Fangio won his fifth World Championship, the classically-proportioned 250F Maserati epitomized the Grand Prix car of the period.

It was developed from the Formula 2 ASSG/6, with a new space frame (which was progressively lightened), gearbox/rear axle unit and de Dion rear end. The engine, enlarged to 2·5 litres, retained the two gear-driven o.h.c., two magnetos (twelve plugs) and the three double-choke Webers of its predecessor. During its active career the factory also experimented with, *inter alia*, streamlining, fuel injection and, half-heartedly, as they were only partly convinced by private British modifications, with disc brakes. Departing from the original design, the 250F/2 (1956) had its engine installed offset and at an angle to the centreline, the transmission passing to the left of the offset cockpit. The 250F/3, a final scaled-down version, appeared after half-completed experiments with a V-12 had been abandoned in 1957.

Fangio won the first two *grandes épreuves* (Argentine and Belgian G.P.s) of the new Formula with the 250F and then left the Scuderia to drive the Mercedes W.196—a move which probably cost Maserati the Championship—and during the rest of that season the car won only six secondary events. In 1955 Mercedes-Benz carried all before them in the *grandes épreuves*, whilst Maserati consolidated their hold on the secondary races, the 250F winning nine.

Moss's victories at Monaco and Monza (250F/2) broke the run of Lancia-Ferrari championship wins in 1956, the Maserati finding the speed to match Ferrari's cars only at the end of the season. Then Fangio returned to Maserati in 1957, winning four *grandes épreuves* (Argentine, Monaco, French and German) and the Constructors' Championship for them.

In a hopeless financial situation, Maserati officially withdrew from racing at the end of 1957. Two 250F/3s were completed for 1958 and, had the character of racing not altered so radically, they might have remained competitive for the rest of the Formula. As it was, they suddenly became obsolete.

SPECIFICATION (250F/1, 1957)

Engine: 6 cylinders; 84 × 75; 2,494 c.c.; twin o.h.c.; max. power: 260 b.h.p. at 7,600 r.p.m. (104 b.h.p. per litre).
Frame: Tubular space-type.
Suspension: Front: independent—unequal-length wishbones, coil springs and anti-roll bar; rear: de Dion axle, sliding guide and radius rods and transverse leaf spring. Hydraulic shock absorbers.
Brakes: Hydraulic drum.
Dimensions: Wheelbase: 7 ft. 6 in.; track, front, 4 ft. 4 in., rear, 4 ft. 2 in.

70 *The outstanding car of the first two seasons of 2·5-litre Grand Prix racing, the W.196 Mercedes-Benz was occasionally beaten, or was lucky to win, in 1954, but convincingly dominated the 1955 Championship. (Moss, the first British driver to win a British Grand Prix, at Aintree, 1955.)*

MERCEDES-BENZ W.196

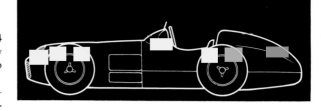

MERCEDES-BENZ RETURNED to Grand Prix racing in 1954 with the W.196, a car bristling with novelty and adequately backed technically and financially. Their reward came in two championships and vast publicity.

The engine was a straight-eight, notable for two features—its use of fuel injection and desmodromic valve gear. Traditionally the cylinders were made in two blocks with integral heads and welded-on water jackets. It was laid almost flat in the space frame. The i.f.s. was conventional; in a new independent system at the rear the drive was taken to the wheels through jointed half-shafts, the hubs being carried on swinging arms centrally pivoted only six inches above ground level. Brakes were mounted inboard front and rear. The car first appeared at Rheims with a fully-streamlined body enclosing the wheels and, as Mercedes shortly found at Silverstone, handicapping the drivers, who were quite unable to accurately judge their line through corners. Thereafter it was used only on high-speed circuits (Avus and Monza). The car was refined in detail in 1955, when short and long wheelbase variants (the former with outboard front brakes) were also built.

In 1954 Mercedes depended for much of their success on Fangio—he drove the winning W.196 in the Grands Prix of France, Germany, Switzerland and Italy; drove the highest-placed Mercedes at Silverstone (4th) and Barcelona (3rd) and ran second to Kling in the Avus G.P. 'demonstration run'. Moss joined the team to give him much-needed backing in 1955, when, except in Argentina, the W.196 raced only in championship events, losing only one of the six run (Monaco, where the cars retired). Fangio won the Argentine, Belgian, Dutch and Italian events (and the Buenos Aires G.P.), shadowed at Spa and Zandvoort by Moss, who led the Mercedes 1, 2, 3, 4 victory in the British G.P. Mercedes-Benz retired from Grand Prix racing at the end of the season and disappeared from the circuits after racing only fourteen times.

SPECIFICATION

Engine: 8 cylinders; 76 × 68·8 mm.; 2,496 c.c.; twin o.h.c.; max. power: 290 b.h.p. at 8.500 r.p.m. (116.2 b.h.p. per litre).

Frame: Tubular space-type.

Suspension: Front: independent—double wishbones and torsion bars; rear: independent—swing axle and torsion bars. Hydraulic shock absorbers.

Brakes: Hydraulic drum, inboard front and rear.

Dimensions: Wheelbase: 7 ft. 0½ in., 7 ft. 3 in. (standard car), *or* 8 ft. 1½ in. (streamlined car, 7 ft. 8½ in.); track, front, 4 ft. 4½ in., rear, 4 ft. 5 in.

72 *The outrigged sponsons of the D50 provided a measure of
streamlining and carried fuel and oil (on the left), thus con-
centrating these variable weights within the wheelbase. Its
handling qualities, however, were odd, and only became
acceptable when Ferrari moved the fuel to the tail. (Ascari,
Monaco, 1955.)*

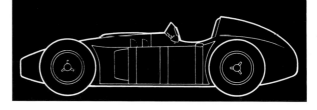

THE SECOND WHOLLY new car built to the 2·5-litre Grand Prix Formula in 1954 was the Lancia D50. Conceived on very different lines to its German rival, it was designed by Vittorio Jano (of pre-war Alfa Romeo fame) and was the Turin firm's first Grand Prix car. It had an ultra-light chassis built up of small-diameter crossbraced tubing, and the front suspension elements were mounted directly on to the engine, which thus became, in effect, a frame member. The compact V-8 engine, initially 73·6 **M** 73·1 mm., (about 260 b.h.p.) had twin o.h.c. per bank and four double-choke downdraught carburetters.

After exhaustive tests at Monza, the D50 was first raced in the 1954 Spanish G.P., showing fantastic acceleration and high speed for nine laps (Ascari raised the Barcelona lap record to 100·97 m.p.h. before retiring). In 1955 the cars had six outings as Lancias: after a fruitless race in Argentina, Ascari won at Naples and Turin, whilst Castellotti finished second at Monaco and Pau. The engine burst in the sole car entered for the Belgian G.P.

Following Ascari's death and the Fiat take-over, Lancia closed their racing department and the D50s, plus a Fiat subsidy, were handed over to Ferrari, whose own Squalos were proving far from satisfactory. Largely unchanged, the Lancia ran at Oulton Park and practised at Monza in the autumn. Ferrari then set about making one good car out of the Squalo and the D50, settling down for the 1956 European season with a team of Lancia-Ferraris. In these cars the fuel was removed to the tail from the outrigged sponsons which were merged into the body; the rear suspension was modified and the front end stiffened with additional cross-bracing. The sponsons disappeared in 1957, when the chassis and rear suspension were also further modified.

The Ferrari team lost only two championship races in 1956, Fangio winning the British and German G.P.s and sharing the winning car in Argentina, whilst Collins won the Belgian and French events. By contrast, the Lancia-Ferraris won only three secondary races (Syracuse, Naples and Rheims) in 1957 before giving way to the Dino Ferraris.

SPECIFICATION (LANCIA-FERRARI)

Engine: 8 cylinders (90° V-8); 76 × 68·5 mm.; 2,490 c.c.; four o.h.c.; max. power: 280 b.h.p. at 8,000 r.p.m. (112 b.h.p. per litre).

Frame: Tubular space-type.

Suspension: Front: independent—twin wishbones, transverse leaf spring and anti-roll bar; rear: de Dion axle, sliding guide and radius rods and transverse leaf spring. Telescopic shock absorbers.

Brakes: Hydraulic drum.

Dimensions: Wheelbase: 7 ft. 6 in.; track, front and rear, 4 ft. 2 in.

74 *Reg Parnell at Oulton Park in September 1955 with the Type B Connaught which Brooks drove to victory in the Syracuse Grand Prix one month later.*

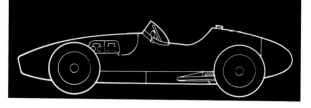

ON OCTOBER 23, 1955, a British driver in a British car won an international Grand Prix for the first time (with one disputed exception) for over thirty years. The driver was Tony Brooks, in his first G.P., the car a 2·5-litre Type B Connaught, and the race at Syracuse, by which name this model was thereafter known. This promising success proved to be the pinnacle of Connaught Engineering's achievements, for shortage of money restricted their activities in 1956, and when Kenneth McAlpine had to withdraw his backing in 1957 their racing came to an end.

The Formula 1 Type B was developed by Rodney Clarke and Mike Oliver from their successful F.2 cars which first ran in 1950. The original 2·5-litre car (1954) had enveloping streamlined bodywork with a distinctive tailfin. However, this proved heavy and vulnerable and was abandoned in favour of the normal open-wheeled type. It had a simple ladder frame of large-diameter tubes, a de Dion rear-axle layout and servo-boosted disc brakes. The Alta engine, worked on by Weslake and by Connaughts, drove through a preselector gearbox mounted in unit with the final drive. Hillborn-Travers fuel injection—pioneered on the F.2 cars—was used on the first Type B and some later cars, with mixed results. As with all Connaughts, right from the early post-war sports cars, their real forté was excellent roadholding.

Despite their shoestring racing budget, the works Connaughts, backed-up by independent cars, were well placed in British secondary events in 1956, but the team raced on the Continent only twice, failing at Syracuse and then outlasting much faster opposition in the European G.P. at Monza to finish third and fifth (Flockhart, Fairman). Their reputation for reliability rather than speed was in a sense misplaced, as it was bought by a deliberate restriction of r.p.m., certain engine parts being known to be fragile. In 1957 a 'dart'-shaped derivative appeared and won its first race (Goodwood, Easter), but Connaught shortly afterwards withdrew from competition. The 'dart' reappeared in a new guise in 1962, entering (unsuccessfully) for the Indianapolis '500'.

SPECIFICATION

Engine: 4 cylinders; 93·6 × 90 mm.; 2,470 c.c.; twin o.h.c.; max. power: 250 b.h.p. at 6,500 r.p.m. (101 b.h.p. per litre).

Frame: Tubular.

Suspension: Front: independent—wishbones and coil springs; rear: de Dion axle, torsion bars and radius rods. Hydraulic shock absorbers.

Brakes: Hydraulic disc.

Dimensions: Wheelbase: 7 ft. 6 in.; track, front and rear, 4 ft. 2 in.

76 *By modern standards the Vanwall was a big and high Grand Prix car, but its body was aerodynamically correct from the start and never needed substantial modification to let un-allowed-for air in or out. (Moss, 1958 British Grand Prix, Silverstone.)*

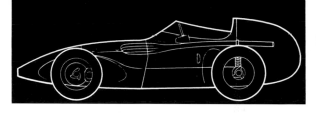

EXASPERATED BY THE confusions of Bourne, G. A. (Tony) Vandervell withdrew his support from the B.R.M. project and in 1950 bought a 4·5-litre Ferrari. As the 'Thinwall Special', this machine provided the main British opposition to the V-16 and also served a useful test-bed purpose. His first hybrid Vanwall (Norton-inspired engine in a Ferrari-type chassis) was originally intended for the Formula 2 Grands Prix of 1953, but did not actually race until Easter 1954.

A 2·5-litre engine was developed from the 1954 unit by L. Kuzmicki and followed Norton motorcycle practice in many ways, consisting of four separate cylinder barrels spigoted to a light-alloy crankcase and cylinder head. The valves were closed by exposed hair-springs and opened by cylindrical tappets running in separate cam-boxes. The carburetters used on the 2-litre and interim 2·3-litre engines were replaced in 1955 by a fuel-injection system, increasing power at some cost in reliability. The 1956 space frame and suspension (further modified at the rear in 1957) were the work of Colin Chapman, and the striking low-drag body was designed by Frank Costin.

In this form the car first raced in the 1956 International Trophy at Silverstone, Moss winning at a record 100·47 m.p.h. Tony Vandervell then concentrated on the *grandes épreuves* and after suffering many setbacks Harry Schell succeeded in finishing among the leaders in the French and Italian G.P.s: his best placing was fourth, at Spa.

Stirling Moss, Tony Brooks, and later, Stuart Lewis-Evans joined the team in 1957. This formidable team with a first-class car won the British G.P. at Aintree, when Moss took over Brook's car, and went on to trounce the Italians at Prescara and Monza. The peak was reached in 1958 when Brooks won the Belgian, German and Italian G.P.s, Moss the Dutch, Portuguese and Morrocan events and brought the Constructors' Championship to Britain for the first time.

SPECIFICATION

Engine: 4 cylinders; 96 × 88 mm.; 2,490 c.c.; twin o.h.c.; max. power: 262 b.h.p. at 7,500 r.p.m. (105·2 b.h.p. per litre).

Frame: Multi-tubular.

Suspension: Front: independent—double wishbones, coil springs and anti-roll bar; rear: de Dion axle and coil springs. Telescopic shock absorbers.

Brakes: Hydraulic disc (inboard at rear).

Dimensions: Wheelbase: 7 ft. 6½ in.; track, front, 4 ft. 5¾ in., rear, 4 ft. 3¾ in.

78 *The essentially simple early F.2 Coopers appeared spindly by comparison with the later low cars. (Brooks, Goodwood Easter Meeting 1957.)*

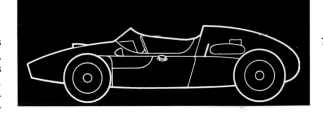

QUICK OFF THE mark when a new, 1·5-litre, Formula 2 was announced in 1956 to come into force the following year, Coopers designed and built a single-seater in a matter of weeks and ran it in the 'trial' F.2 event at the 1956 British G.P. meeting. It won handsomely from an assorted field of sports-racing machines, a victory whose promise was completely fulfilled when Coopers took the international Constructors' Championship in all three years that it was functioning (1958–59–60).

Whereas Cooper's previous F.2 model was a sidestep from their traditional path of design (its Bristol engine was at the front), the 1956 car stemmed directly from the rear-engined Formula 3 and sports-racing models. The Coventry Climax FWB engine was mounted behind the driver in a frame welded-up from curved and angled steel tubes. Front and rear independent suspension was by transverse leaf springs and wishbones, and cast magnesium-alloy 'solid-spoke' wheels were an unusual feature that soon became a Cooper commonplace. Four of these stubby little cars were built and won every race they entered in 1956.

For 1957 the 'over-square' twin-o.h.c. Coventry Climax FPF was ready, producing over 30 b.h.p. more than the single-cam unit. To take it, the Cooper was lengthened by 2 in., while the body was lowered and widened to accommodate three larger fuel tanks. Nine twin-o.h.c. cars were laid down and, although initially subject to engine and gearbox troubles, were running well by the end of the season. The 1958 car (virtual twin of a F.1 version) had a lower, wider body, sturdier gearbox and coil-spring front suspension. Largely in private owners' hands, Coopers won ten of the thirteen major F.2 races in that year. The Championship fell to them again in 1959 (when two privately-owned cars were fitted with twin-o.h.c. Borgward engines). In the last year of the 1·5-litre Formula 2 they completed the hat-trick (sharing the Championship with Porsche) and a unique double, capturing both F.1 and F.2 Constructors' Championships in two successive years.

SPECIFICATION

Engine: 4 cylinders; 81·2 × 71·7 mm.; 1,475 c.c.; twin o.h.c.; max. power: 145 b.h.p. at 7,500 r.p.m. (98·3 b.h.p. per litre).

Frame: Multi-tubular.

Suspension: Front: independent—coil springs and wishbones; rear; independent—transverse leaf spring and wishbones. Hydraulic shock absorbers.

Brakes: Hydraulic drum (disc optional).

Dimensions: Wheelbase: 7 ft. 7 in.; track, front, 3 ft. 9½ in., rear, 3 ft. 11 in.

80 *Under its low exterior—somewhat spoiled by the obtrusive cockpit—the Belond AP Special differed only in detail from its Indianapolis contemporaries. Oddly, to European eyes, the driver wears a safety harness and has no mirrors. (Bryan, Monza, 1958.)*

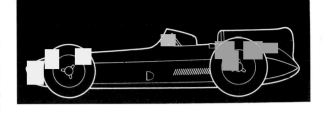

AMERICAN TRACK-RACING cars are often thought of as relics from the backwoods when compared with European road-racing machines. Certainly this somewhat sterile type of racing does encourage the retention of some rather odd features: the tracks have fairly constant-radius turns to the left only, therefore the weight distribution of the cars is biased and sophisticated suspension systems are an unnecessary complication; rolling starts require only the simplest of transmissions; and the nature of the racing makes little demand upon brakes so that these components on cars weighing upwards of three-quarters of a ton would seem inadequate on a self-respecting European Junior. Nevertheless, the cars are well suited to their job; far from crude; very, very fast and, as some rather surprised Europeans witnessed at Monza in 1957 and 1958, controllable to within fine limits.

After a post-war burst of enthusiastic unorthodoxy—experiments with front-wheel drive and blown engines, for example—Indianapolis machines increasingly conformed to standard during the fifties. Indeed, no entries not powered by the classic Meyer and Drake Offenhauser four-cylinder engine managed to qualify for the 1959 race. Generally common design features during this period were a tubular frame; rigid front axle and live rear axle without a differential; an Offenhauser 'four', normally installed offset to the left of the chassis centre-line, and a cockpit offset to the right with the transmission running alongside it.

Minor variations on this basic design theme are, of course, common. One of the most successful cars in recent years has been the Belond AP Special with which Jimmy Bryan won at Indianapolis in 1957 and 1958 and took second place in the 1958 Monza 500-mile race, leaving the lap record for the banked circuit at 174·76 m.p.h. This car had an almost horizontal engine installation, making it one of the lowest Indianapolis machines ever built (bonnet height 22 in.), but in most other respects it was representative of recent practice in the highly specialized school of American track racers.

SPECIFICATION

Engine: 4 cylinders; 107 × 114 mm.; 4,200 c.c.; twin o.h.c.; max. power: 375 b.h.p. at 6,500 r.p.m. (89·3 b.h.p. per litre).

Frame: Tubular.

Suspension: Front: rigid axle and torsion bars; rear: live axle and torsion bars. Hydraulic shock absorbers (2 per wheel).

Brakes: Hydraulic disc.

Dimensions: Wheelbase: 8 ft.; track, 4 ft. 4 in.

82 *Mike Hawthorn at Silverstone in 1958. His car always had a small flat screen (normally the Dino 246 had a smooth wrap-round). Plastics carburetter intake covers were later used and the broad ribbed drum brakes gave way to discs in 1959.*

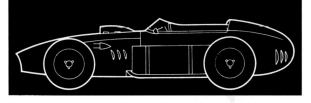

THE DINO 246 supplanted Ferrari's Lancia-based cars in 1958; two years later it was the only front-line G.P. car still adhering to the traditional front-engined layout. Named 'Dino' after Enzo Ferrari's son ('24' for the capacity, '6' for the number of cylinders), these compact and purposeful cars provided the only serious opposition to British cars during the closing seasons of the 2·5-litre Formula. Driving them, Mike Hawthorn became the first British Champion Driver of the World in 1958.

The car first appeared in Formula 2 guise (1·5-litre '156') at Naples in 1957 and at the end of that season a 2·4-litre version was raced at Casablanca. The V-6 engine was designed from the outset to run on petrol (obligatory fuel for the Grands Prix, 1958–60). Its two cylinder blocks were cast in one unit with the crankcase, and alternative types had one or two overhead camshafts to each block, the former giving better low-speed torque, the latter greater power. An enlarged engine, the '256', was also seen occasionally. A divided propeller shaft carried the drive to a combined clutch, gearbox and final drive.

Two basic chassis were used concurrently, the original 'F.2 type' and a redesigned and stronger type, lengthened in 1959 as Ferrari experimented to improve roadholding. The suspension was also progressively modified, the original de Dion layout at the rear eventually being replaced by an independent swing-axle design.

The Dino 246 almost held its own in 1958. Although it only won two *grandes épreuves*, the French (Hawthorn) and British (Collins) Grands Prix, it took seven second and five third places and made the fastest lap in six. It was outclassed by the Coopers on all but the fastest circuits in 1959, again winning only two *grandes épreuves* (at Rheims—Brooks's race speed 127·45 m.p.h.—and on the artificial Avus circuit—Brooks's race speed 143·61 m.p.h.). Ferrari was content to mark time in 1960, his completely outmoded cars gaining only one rather hollow victory against scratch opposition in the Italian G.P.

SPECIFICATION

Engine: 6 cylinders (60° V-6); 85 × 71 mm.; 2,417 c.c.; four o.h.c.; max. power: 280 b.h.p. at 8,500 r.p.m. (115·8 b.h.p. per litre).

Frame: Tubular space-type.

Suspension: Front: independent—transverse wishbones, coil springs and anti-roll bars; rear: independent—swing axle, transverse wishbones and coil spring/damper units. Telescopic shock absorbers.

Brakes: Hydraulic disc.

Dimensions: Wheelbase: 7 ft. 7½ in.; track, front, 4 ft., rear, 3 ft. 11 in.

84 *By 1960 the Cooper had the measure of its opponents on even the fastest circuits and had developed into a low, lithe machine which was seldom beaten. (Brabham, 1960 Belgian Grand Prix, Spa.)*

COOPER 2·5-litre

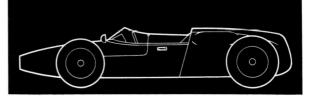

UNQUESTIONABLY THE MOST successful Grand Prix car that Britain has ever produced, the 2·5-litre Formula 1 Cooper-Climax took over where Vanwall left off. It brought the Constructors' Championship to this country twice running, provided the mount for Jack Brabham's two World Championships, initiated a design trend followed almost without exception in Europe, and even influenced American track-racing car design. In 1958–59 the Cooper was the only rear-engined G.P. contender, but within three years the front-engined car had virtually vanished from the field.

The Formula 1 Cooper grew out of the 1·5-litre F.2 model by easy stages. At the instigation of the Coopers, *père et fils*, and R. R. C. Walker, Coventry Climax built a 1·9-litre version of their 1,475 c.c. FPF engine in 1957. Two cars with this 175 b.h.p. 1,960-c.c. unit ran without success in Continental events—although Brabham won the Boxing Day *Formule Libre* race at Brands Hatch—but in 1958 Moss won the Argentine G.P. with this car against strong 2·5-litre opposition. Although the only other G.P. to fall to Cooper that year (Trintignant, Monaco) was won with this same car, full 1958 models with 195 b.h.p. 2·2-litre engines, disc brakes and a wider body ran promisingly throughout the season.

In 1959 the Grand Prix Cooper really arrived. The full 2·5-litre Climax engine developing about 240 b.h.p. was normally installed, though independently modified cars had B.R.M., Ferrari and Maserati engines. Brabham and McLaren in works four-speed cars, and Moss and Trintignant in Walker's privately entered five-speed models, all had intermittent transmission trouble, but nonetheless won the Championship with five *grandes épreuves* between them.

With one of the 1959 cars McLaren won the 1960 Argentine G.P., but for the European season two lower cars with five-speed gearboxes and all-round coil suspension were run by the works. With them Brabham won five *grandes épreuves* in a row (Dutch, Belgian, French, British and Portuguese G.P.s). In all, ten major Grands Prix fell to Cooper that year.

SPECIFICATION

Engine: 4 cylinders; 94 × 89·9 mm.; 2,495 c.c.; twin o.h.c.; max. power: 245 b.h.p. at 6,750 r.p.m. (98·2 b.h.p. per litre).

Frame: Multi-tubular space-type.

Suspension: Front: independent—coil springs and wishbones; rear: independent—coil springs and wishbones. Hydraulic shock absorbers.

Brakes: Hydraulic disc.

Dimensions: Wheelbase: 7 ft. 7 in.; track, front, 3 ft. 10½ in., rear, 4 ft.

Brilliantly successful in its first racing season, the 'chunky' Lotus 18 not only ran away with most British races but completely overshadowed the previously-dominant Italian cars on the Continent. (J. Clark, 1960 Stuttgart Grand Prix, Solitude.)

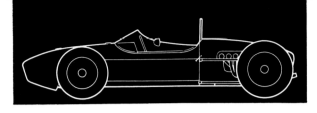

FORMULA JUNIOR WAS conceived in Italy as a cadet class, the cars to be monopostos using many components from standard production vehicles, and achieved international status in 1959. During that year it slowly caught on in Britain and several British constructors turned to Juniors among them Colin Chapman, whose first rear-engined car, the Lotus 18, was to dominate the Formula in its first racing season.

The formula set upper capacity limits to 1,100 c.c. (minimum car weight 400 kg.) or 1,000 c.c. (minimum weight 360 kg.). In common with virtually all 1959–60 British Juniors, the Lotus 18 was built to the lower weight limit, with a modified Ford 105E engine in all but three of the 125 cars built. Most of these power units were tuned by Cosworth Engineering Ltd., whose extensive modifications almost doubled the output of the engine. The car had a very rigid multi-tubular frame, weighing only 60 lb., and a removable glass-fibre body.

The Team Lotus cars, driven by top-flight drivers, were almost unbeatable in 1960, but, more often than not, their closest challengers were also driving Lotus 18s. Although officially replaced by a new car, the Lotus 20, in 1961, the 18 remained competitive in a class where driving abilities varied widely, skill often compensating for the 'obsolescence' of the car.

With a 2·5-litre Coventry Climax engine, disc brakes and other minor differences, the 18 was also the 1960 Lotus G.P. car. In this role it was raced by Team Lotus and by independents, but in the *grandes épreuves* was rather overshadowed by the Coopers. Before and after recovery from his accident at Spa, which for a time made the Lotus suspension suspect, Stirling Moss won the Monaco and American Grands Prix in Rob Walker's car. Fitted with a 1·5-litre engine and an improved body, the Walker Lotus became the only car to beat the Ferraris in 1961, when Moss drove it to brilliant victories in the Monaco and German Grands Prix.

SPECIFICATION (LOTUS 18 JUNIOR)

Engine: (Cosworth-modified Ford 105E): 4 cylinders; 80·96 × 48·41 mm.; 997 c.c.; pushrod o.h.v.; max. power: 75 b.h.p. at 7,200 r.p.m. (75 b.h.p. per litre).

Frame: Multi-tubular space-type.

Suspension: Front: independent—wishbones, coil spring/damper units and anti-roll bar; rear: independent—lower wishbone, radius rod, fixed-length articulated drive shaft and coil spring/damper units. Telescopic shock absorbers.

Brakes: Hydraulic drum.

Dimensions: Wheelbase: 7 ft. 6 in.; track, front, 4 ft. 1 in., rear, 3 ft. 11 in.

The wide-bodied, narrow-tracked Ferrari was the only 1961 G.P. car to use wire wheels. The twin plastic blisters over the carburetter intakes indentify the 120° car; the 65° engine had a larger single blister. (Hill, 1961 German Grand Prix, Nürburgring.)

FERRARI 1·5-litre

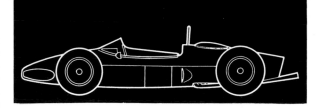

AFTER THE BARREN closing years of the 2·5-litre Formula, Ferrari bounced back to dominate the Grands Prix of 1961. Maranello self-sufficiency—Sefac Ferrari rely far less on 'bought-out' components than most British constructors—meant that a new Ferrari was ready for the new Formula. British contenders wasted precious development time while futile efforts were made to rescind the 1·5-litre Formula.

The 1961 Grand Prix Ferrari appeared to have much in common with its Formula 2 predecessor, but was, in fact, a new car. Two engines were used, a 65° V-6 developed from the F.2 Dino 156 and a new 120° V-6. The wide vee of the latter helped to lower the car's centre of gravity and solved problems of balance at high r.p.m. (but initially restricted oil circulation). Each bank had two overhead camshafts, while two three-choke carburetters fed the cylinders individually through almost vertical pipes. The gearbox was mounted behind the rear axle with the clutch exposed in the tail, above it being the starter required by the formula. The space frame was based on four large-diameter tubes, the engine itself providing some stiffening.

As the season opened a solitary 65° car, driven by the relatively inexperienced Giancarlo Baghetti, administered a salutary shock to the British and German *équipes* at Syracuse. In the *grandes épreuves*, the Ferraris were beaten only twice—on the driver's circuits of Monaco (Ferrari second, third, fourth) and Nürburgring (Ferrari second, third) by an on-top-of-form Moss—whilst the works team retired at Rheims, leaving Baghetti to win in the 'independent' FISA car. Ferraris were first and second at Zandvoort; took first placces at Spa; the first three at Aintree, and won at Monza. Driving them, Phil Hill became World Champion Driver.

The cars reappeared in 1962, some experimentally-modified (with, e.g., rear track increased by 6 in. or gearbox installed ahead of rear axle). Still deficient in roadholding and matched by the new British V-8s in the power race, the Ferraris were nevertheless reliable and finished third and fourth in the Dutch and Belgian G.P.s, and second and third at Monaco.

SPECIFICATION

Engine: 6 cylinders (120° V-6); 73 × 58·8 mm.; 1,476 c.c.; four o.h.c.; max. power: 190 b.h.p. at 9,500 r.p.m. (129 b.h.p. per litre).

Frame: Tubular space-type.

Suspension: Front: independent—double wishbones and coil spring/damper units; rear: independent—double wishbones and coil spring/damper units. Telescopic shock absorbers.

Brakes: Hydraulic disc, outboard front, inboard rear.

Dimensions: Wheelbase: 7 ft. 6½ in.; track, 4 ft. 0½ in.